Acknowledgements.

I began to write this cookbook in 1994 with recipes from my family in England.

Since then I have gathered many fabulous recipes from historic hotels, inns and restaurants from the British Isles to whom I extend my heartfelt appreciation.

Special thanks to Michael Thompstone, a fellow 'Brit', without whose time, creativity, dedication and computer expertise, this book would never have been completed.

A big round of applause goes to another 'Brit', Kenneth Mee for helping to convert the British recipes from lbs/grams, pints/litres to American and to proof read every line.

Last, but not least, my love and appreciation goes to Bill Ewing for encouraging and inspiring me to write the book in the first place.

The author cannot be held responsible for errors in establishments' phone and fax numbers etc.

ISBN 0-9763714-0-5

Derivation of the word Posh

"Oh yes, Mater, we had a posh time of it down there." So in *Punch* for September 25, 1918, do we find the first recorded instance of *posh,* meaning "smart and fashionable." A popular theory holds that it is derived from the initials of "Port Out, Starboard Home," the cooler, and thus more expensive, side of ships traveling between England and India in the mid-19th century. The acronym *POSH* was supposedly stamped on the tickets of first-class passengers traveling on that side of ships owned by the Peninsular and Oriental Steam Navigation Company. No known evidence supports this theory, however. Another word *posh* was 19th- and early 20th-century British slang for "money," specifically "a halfpenny, cash of small value." This word is borrowed from the Romany word *påsh,* "half," which was used in combinations such as *påshera,* "halfpenny." *Posh,* also meaning "a dandy," is recorded in two dictionaries of slang, published in 1890 and 1902, although this particular *posh* may be still another word. This word or these words are, however, much more likely to be the source of *posh* than "Port Out, Starboard Home," although the latter source certainly has caught the public's etymological fancy.

(from Dictionary.com)

CONTENTS

PUB GRUB AND POSH BRITISH FARE

Contrary to popular belief, not all English meals are tasteless and overcooked. In fact, British pub-grub has become somewhat of an institution, perhaps because it is normally accompanied by conviviality, a glass of sherry, shandy or a pint of bitter.

Pub-grub meals are designed to offer speedy service for lunch, or the after work crowd who stop off for a pint and a bite to eat on their way home.

Elegant country houses and old coaching inns in Britain offer more elaborate menus than public houses. The Posh Fare recipes were sent to me by gracious owners of historic hotels and country house restaurants in various parts of the British Isles. Some are wonderfully simple recipes and others are rather sumptuous. I have included a little history of each of these wonderful establishments, which I hope you will find of interest.

I have written about the pub meals I remember and included some home recipes which have been passed down through the generations and are linked with an old fashioned way of life when the lady of the house took more time to prepare lunch and cook cakes and pastries for afternoon tea.

I had to make a few adaptations since some ingredients are not available in this country. However, I believe I have succeeded in keeping the majority of the recipes authentic and the measurement conversions accurate.

Please enjoy this sample taste of Britain, and if you will forgive the intrusion of a little French, may I wish you bon appétit.

Angela Ewing

A Brief History Of Public Houses

A "Public House" is defined in the dictionary as a British inn, tavern or hostelry. The Romans built the first taverns when they occupied Britain in A.D. 84. When they first arrived they settled around the east Kent coast before moving inland. Today, Kent is still a major area for growing hops, which are used to flavor beer. Hopbines and strange looking buildings called Oast Houses where the hops are dried are still an integral part of the Kentish landscape.

In 1393 King Richard II made a law that all inns must have signs. Since many of the population were illiterate at that time, it was easier to have a picture sign that reflected the customs of the area.

In the country, pubs use signs like "The Old Bull" or "The Plough". In a city pub you are more likely to find signs that suggests allegiance to royalty. When Henry VII married Elizabeth of York, pubs displaying "Rose and Crown" signs became very popular. Only upon the death of Queen Victoria in 1901 was it permitted to paint inn signs with her picture.

Pub Signs

Signs often depict whether or not the inn, tavern or hostelry is owned by a brewery or by an independent innkeeper. "Free House" means that the innkeeper is the sole owner of the establishment and can sell any beer he chooses. If the sign has a name underneath such as "Courage" or "Whitbread" the pub is owned by that brewery and managed by the innkeeper who cannot sell beer from any other brewery.

Free House   *Owned by*
                                Whitbread
                                Brewery

These days not all pubs are inns and not all inns have accommodations, but at one time the old coaching inns always had rooms for rent and were the forerunners of today's hotels and motels.

"Time Gentlemen Please"

In England, public houses used to be open from noon until 2:00 pm and then 5:00 pm until 10:30 pm or 11:00 pm. Recently, however, the laws have been changed to allow them to be open all day, depending on the whim of the landlord or the owner. The latest time to order a drink is 10:50pm to allow the pub to close at 11:00pm.

Thirsty customers often make the mistake of arriving just before closing time only to hear the barman or barmaid announce, "Last orders please", or worse, "Time gentlemen please." If the publican is found to be serving after hours, the law can legally close his establishment or demand a heavy fine.

In England, Ireland, Scotland and Wales, large numbers of Public Houses abound, for they are as much a part of the British way of life today as they were in the first century.

In almost every country village, nestled next to the cake shop, butcher or confectioners--and usually across the street from the church--you will find a little pub with its colorful sign swinging in the wind above the cobbled street.

There's nothing quite like an old coaching inn for atmosphere. Most have been preserved and are still very grand with heavy half-timbered archways, overhanging balconies and massive wooden doors. Sitting in front of a roaring fire you can almost hear the coach and horses rumble into the courtyard to drop off mail or a cold and weary traveler.

Town pubs often lack the ambiance of older historical country inns, but today's meals are quite sophisticated compared to the uninteresting sandwiches and chicken-and-chips that were served in the early sixties.

Ordering food in a Pub

There is no single correct way to order a meal or snack in a pub. Different pubs have different systems for ordering food: some take meal orders at the bar, others have separate counters for food. Some pubs have menus on the tables; others have menus on the bar counter or chalked on blackboards – or both.

Wherever and however food is served, drinks must almost always be purchased at the bar, so the best strategy is to go up to the bar first, order your drinks and ask the bar staff what the procedure is for ordering food.

Even if your food is brought to you at your table, the no-waiter-service rule will probably still apply to drinks, so do not expect the staff who bring your food to take orders for drinks as well. You may find this custom irritating, but try to appreciate the opportunities it gives you for friendly chats with the bar staff and other natives. Pubs are not just about food and drink: pubs are about sociability, and every trip to the bar to buy drinks is another chance to make contact.

Tourist mistake: *A Japanese couple looked at the 'bar snacks menu' and ordered five dishes each, thinking that a 'bar snack' must be the British equivalent of a tiny sushi-bar portion. In British pubs, a bar snack is a simple, one-item meal – such as a sandwich, a pizza, a pork pie, etc. – but it is still a meal, not a nibble! In a small, quiet pub, the bar staff would have realized that the order must be a mistake, but this unfortunate couple happened to be in a very large, busy pub, where the staff assumed that they were ordering for a group of ten.*

Ordering beer: the basics

Simply asking for "a beer" in a British pub is a bit like asking for "a wine" in a French restaurant. There are hundreds of different varieties of beer available, each with its own distinctive taste and characteristics. Pubs often have a range of around 20 different beers behind the bar, many of them on draught (on tap), some in bottles and a few in cans. They range from dark stouts, through mild ales and bitter to lager – a light, gold-colored beer. (You would normally get lager if you just asked for a beer in most other countries, including Europe, the United States and Australia.) In Scotland, bitter is described as 'heavy' or '70/-' (Seventy Shilling Ale).

Don't worry – you don't have to become a connoisseur to enjoy British beer. At a basic level, the bar staff just need to know whether you want bitter, lager or another sort of beer, and whether you want a pint, a half, or one of the wide variety of imported and domestic beers sold by the bottle (look at the glass-fronted coolers and shelves behind the bar to see what bottled beers are available).

A pint is 0.568 litres (i.e. quite a big drink). 'A half' means a half-pint. The 'pint' element is silent. When ordering, you just say "A half of lager, please" or "A half of bitter, please". This is very often shortened to "Half a lager, please" and so on. The 'please' is important.

If you are interested, there is a lot more to find out about the endless different varieties of traditional British beers. Some publicans and bar staff are very knowledgeable, and will be happy – when they are not too busy serving the stuff – to explain it all to you.

Regional variation: *In Northern Ireland, pub goers tend to order beer by brand name: they will say "A pint of Harp", rather than "A pint of lager" and "A pint of Smithwicks" rather than "A pint of bitter". You may also hear the Irish asking for "A glass of Harp" or "A glass of Guinness". In Northern Ireland, 'a glass' means 'a half'. To confuse you, there is also a tradition, mainly among older drinkers in Northern Ireland, of referring to a shot of Whiskey as "A half 'un". You may also hear this expression in Scotland, where it should not be mistaken for "A half", which, as in England and Wales, means 'a half-pint'.*

Acknowledgements: Social Issues Research Centre

<u>England - *Beer from the pub.*</u>

Bass Pale Ale - *Brewed since 1777 by Bass Brewers Limited, this English ale has a reputation of excellence in Burton-on-Trent, England.*

Double Diamond Original Burton Ale - *Having an international hop character, this British beer has a full malt flavor that is very drinkable.*

Fuller's ESB English Ale - *Known as the best British beer around, ESB is brewed from pale ale, crystal malts and various hops to produce what is the definitive premium ale.*

Fuller's London Pride Traditional English Beer - *Fuller's flagship brand, London Pride is the official bitter of British*

Airways and has a good malty base with well-developed hop flavors from many varieties of hops.

John Courage Amber Premium Beer - *This amber colored ale has a full bodied, sweet taste and a roasty, hoppy palate, combining to create a complex, malty, session beer.*

Mackeson Triple Stout - *This milk stout is brewed to have a wonderfully smooth and thick consistency, with a rich sweetness of flavor reminiscent of chocolate milk.*

Newcastle Brown Ale - *Brewed in the oldest beer-making city in England, Newcastle Brown Ale is a mixture of two ales, a strong dark brew and a lighter blend. Incorporating pale ale and crystal malts, and brewed with English bittering hops, this ale is the city of Newcastle's main icon.*

Samuel Smith's Imperial Stout - *Originally brewed for great Champagne connoisseurs, Imperial Stout has a rich, flavorful taste.*

Samuel Smith's Nut Brown Ale - *This brown ale is a walnut-covered specialty, and is often used as a festivity beer, brewed in one of the oldest English brewing styles.*

Samuel Smith's Oatmeal Stout - *A classic stout from the Samuel Smith's Old Brewery, Oatmeal Stout is brewed with a style that recently underwent major changes in 1980. By brewing sweet roasted malts with choice hops, a very dark brown stout beer is produced with a smooth, creamy taste and slightly nutty finish.*

Samuel Smith's Pure Brewed Lager Beer - *Samuel Smith, most famous for their classic ales, offer what is known as "England's finest lager."*

Samuel Smith's Taddy Porter - *This classic English porter is brewed using a combination of caramel and roasted malts, bittering hops and other premium ingredients to produce a roasty oaty malt with a slightly fruity taste.*

Watneys Cream Stout - *This brew's engaging flavor offers an interesting mix of coffee, mocha and faint alcohol while creating a dynamic light-weight stout.*

Whitbread Ale - *This traditional ale has been brewing since 1742 and uses the highest grade of malted barley and choice English hops to produce one of England's finest pale ales.*

Culinarily Speaking, Americans Don't Use English

As Winston Churchill once remarked, "We are two peoples separated by a common language"!

These are just a few of the differences in American and British English terms, which I have called "Kitchen English."

Au Jus is Gravy
Beets are Beetroot
Biscuits are Scones
Bouillon is Stock
Can is Tin
Chips are Crisps
Cilantro is Coriander
Cooked Oatmeal is Porridge (also doing time in prison!)
Cookies are Biscuits
Corn is Maize
Corn Starch is Corn flour
Cream of Wheat is Semolina
Cupcakes are Fairy Cakes
Desserts are Sweets (Candies are Sweets too!)
Egg Plant is Aubergine
English Muffin: there is no such thing!
Fillet (fillay) is Fillet (fill it)
French Fries are Chips
Fruit based drink concentrates are called Squash
Fruit Pits are Stones (14 lbs is also a Stone!)
Golden Raisins are Sultanas
Green Onions or Scallions are Spring Onions

(continued)

(Kitchen English, continued)

Hamburger Bun is a Bap
Hamburger is Minced Meat
Jacket Potato is Baked Potato
Jello is Jelly
Jelly is Jam
Jelly Roll is Swiss Roll
Ketchup is Tomato Sauce
Liquors are Spirits
Mardi Gras (Shrove Tuesday) is Pancake Day
Molasses is Treacle
Napkins are Serviettes (vive la France)
Pancakes are Crêpes (very thin)
Pork Rinds are Pork Scratchings
Porterhouse Steak is Sirloin Steak
Potato Pancakes are Fritters
Powdered Sugar is Icing Sugar
Puddings are often savoury
Sandwich is a Butty (or Sarnie)
Sausages are Bangers (as in Bangers and Mash)
Serve Dinner is to Dish Up
Sirloin is Rump Steak
Slice of Bacon is a Rasher
Squash is Marrow
String Beans are Runner Beans
Stuffing made with meat is Forcemeat
Sunday Roast is a Joint
The English have an "H" on their herbs
To Broil food is to Grill it
Zucchini is Courgette (those French again)

BREAKFAST

Unlike the Continental breakfast with rolls and coffee, or tea, traditional British breakfasts are hearty with two or three courses. Grapefruit or prunes are usually served first, followed by a fish course, such as Finnan Haddie (see page 21) with eggs, or kippers with brown bread and butter. Alternatively, eggs prepared in a variety of ways with an accompaniment of grilled tomatoes, sausage, bacon, mushrooms and black pudding* are served. Breakfast is always rounded off with toast and orange marmalade.

The following breakfast dishes are a little different and well worth trying.

*Note: black pudding is made from pig's blood and fat, and even though it sounds terrible is quite delicious. You really should try this at least once.

Tinakilly Country House and Restaurant, County Wicklow, Ireland.

Tinakilly Country House is twice blessed. The only thing better than discovering a wonderful country retreat by the sea just 30 miles south of Dublin is to discover it has great food as well.

Tinakilly Country House and Restaurant in County Wicklow in Ireland is truly unique. This gracious Victorian style house was built for Captain Halpin, the man who, as commander of the Great Eastern, laid the first successful transatlantic telegraph cable in 1866. A secret hideaway on the doorstep of Dublin, this country house hotel presents superior standards in a peaceful rural environment overlooking the sea. Today the gracious Victorian Italianate style and serenity of Tinakilly provide a soothing respite for those seeking wonderful fresh food in elegant period surroundings. The award-winning kitchen prepares splendid cuisine from fresh local produce and Tinakilly's own herb garden.

Tinakilly is located 29 miles south of Dublin City.

Phone: 011 353 404 69274,   Fax: 011 353 404 67806

Potato and Leek Galettes

from Tinakilly Country House and Restaurant, County
Wicklow, Ireland

For the Galettes:
   1 lb cooked potatoes
   ½ cup finely sliced leek
   ¼ cup finely sliced shallot
   ½ cup melted, unsalted butter,
   salt, pepper and olive oil to fry

Peel and grate the cooked potatoes and place in a bowl. Sauté
the leek and shallots in ¼ cup butter until soft. Add the potato.
Add the remaining melted butter and season the mixture.
Shape the Galettes into 2 ½ inch rounds by ¾ inch high. Fry in
olive oil until crisp and golden. Place under a hot grill to glaze.
Serve with a poached egg and Hollandaise. Garnish the dish
with fresh chervil.

Hollandaise Sauce
   4 crushed peppercorns
   2 tablespoons white wine vinegar
   1 shallot, diced
   2 egg yolks
   1 cup butter, melted
   salt and pepper to taste

Place peppercorns, vinegar and shallots in a pan and reduce
almost completely. Add the egg yolks and beat over a pan of
boiling water until double in volume and thick. Pour in the
warm melted butter in a steady stream, whisking continuously.
Season with salt and pepper.

Chicken Liver Scramble

4 chicken livers, chopped finely
¼ cup butter
4 eggs
4 slices whole-wheat toast
¼ teaspoon salt
¼ teaspoon pepper
parsley and tomatoes as garnish

Put the eggs and seasonings in a blender for 30 seconds. Heat the butter in skillet, add chicken livers, cook for a few seconds then add the eggs and scramble lightly. Serve with triangular pieces of toast and garnish with sliced tomatoes and parsley. This is ideal for lunch as well as breakfast.

Cheese Eggs Soufflé

4 eggs
¼ cup butter
2 tablespoons thin cream
½ cup grated cheddar cheese
salt and pepper to taste.
Oven 350F

Separate the egg yolks from the whites and whisk the whites until stiff. Grease 4 small ovenproof dishes. Beat the yolks with the cream, season with salt and pepper and fold into the egg whites. Bake for 10 minutes on the top shelf of the oven. Sprinkle the cheese over the top for the last 5 minutes of cooking.

Serve on toast with sliced tomatoes.

This is also delicious with chopped ham instead of cheese.

Finnan Haddie

Smoked haddock is hard to find in some areas but it is well worth the search.

It is best to soak the smoked haddock overnight in a bowl of water because it might be salty.

Melt a little butter in a large frying pan and add the fish. Add a mixture of milk and water (½ and ½) until the fish is just covered. Simmer for about 10 minutes, or until the fish flakes easily with a fork.

Place on hot plates in a warm oven and poach the eggs in the remaining water/milk.

Place a poached egg on top of each haddock portion and serve with brown bread or toast and butter.

Kippers

Kippers are smoked herrings and not often found in the States. Sometimes grocery stores import them vacuum-packed from Canada.

Kippers may be baked for about 20 minutes in a regular oven with a little butter, or fried with butter and a little water, covered.

A delicious dish that is very nutritious, served with brown (wheat) bread and butter.

Mixed Grill

Serves 4
4 tablespoons oil
1 sirloin steak approx 8 oz.
4 slices bacon
4 sausages
8 ounces of beef liver
2 tomatoes
4 eggs
¼ cup flour with pinch of salt and pepper
2 teaspoons butter or margarine

Broil or fry the bacon and sausages. Drain on paper towel and put in a warm oven. Fry steak in oil or cook under broiler, until medium rare.

Fry liver separately after dipping lightly in seasoned flour. Turn after one minute and cook one minute longer until just done.

Halve the tomato, spread with butter and sprinkle with breadcrumbs. Broil until soft, about 4 minutes. Fry the egg and baste.

Divide into four and serve on warm plates, with hot buttered toast.

To vary, mushrooms can be added; in this dish it seems anything goes!

Needless to say this is a meat lover's delight and quantities of steak etc. should be kept small.

This dish is also great for dinner.

Milford Hall Hotel, Salisbury, Wiltshire

Milford hall was originally built as a graceful Georgian mansion house and has subsequently been sympathetically extended and modernized without losing any of its character or charm. It successfully combines traditional English hospitality with modern facilities.

The hotel's restaurant has a great reputation for the standard of its cuisine and offers an imaginative menu.

Salisbury is a very interesting place to visit, not only for the town itself, but also for its close proximity to Salisbury Plain and Stonehenge. Winchester, with its famous cathedral that houses King Arthur's Round Table, is only minutes away from Salisbury.

Phone: 011 44 1722 417411   Fax: 011 44 0722 419444

Smoked Haddock Benedict

from Chef Christopher Gilber, Milford Hall Hotel, Salisbury, Wiltshire

Serves 2
2 4-ounce smoked haddock fillets
1 English Muffin, halved
2 eggs
4 rashers of bacon
Butter for muffin

Christopher's Hollandaise Sauce

2 egg yolks
½ cup white wine vinegar
1 bay leaf
8 black peppercorns
¼ cup clarified butter

First make the sauce:
If you don't possess a double boiler, place a glass bowl over a pan of very hot water. Break the eggs into the bowl and whisk until they turn pale. Meanwhile reduce the white wine vinegar in a pan with the peppercorns and bay leaf until about a tablespoon full is left. Pass the vinegar through a sieve and whisk this into the eggs. Gradually add the clarified butter.

Broil the haddock for 4 – 5 minutes until it is just firm. Don't overcook the fish. Fry the bacon and roll in paper towel to remove excess fat. Toast the muffin. Poach eggs in a pan of water with a teaspoon of vinegar until firm but not hard cooked.

Spread the muffin with butter; place bacon then haddock on the muffin and the poached egg on top. Next, spoon the hollandaise sauce over and garnish with a sprig of parsley.

A wholesome, protein-rich breakfast.

Ethnic Dishes

As with most hotels and restaurants in England, pub menus have been adapted to suit an ever-changing society and to reflect new habits and population growth.

Travel has influenced eating habits and viewpoints. Menus and recipes from other countries have found their way into one of the most revered institutions: the British pub.

At one time no Englishman would consider eating rice in any dish other than rice pudding, but today, curry dishes, which arrived in England with the immigrants from India, compete with the proverbial fish and chips. Likewise, Paella, brought back from Spain is a favorite complete meal served in many households and in pubs, as are hamburger and pizza.

LUNCH

Since most working men in Britain at one time had two hours for lunch, (wives didn't work of course), it was customary to serve the main meal between 12:00 noon and 2:00 pm. Hot dinner type meals were usually served at lunchtime; sandwiches were for teatime at 4:00 o'clock and a light supper when the men got home from work around 7:00 pm. Welsh Rarebit (page 40) or Cheese & Onion Hotpot (page 99) were popular in my family.

Menus never varied much from week to week.

Weekday lunches included meals such as leftover Sunday roast served with Bubble and Squeak (see page 91), pork chops and vegetables and the ever-present gravy (au jus), Stew, Shepherd's Pie, Lancashire Hotpot casserole, and Fridays of course would be fish.

Sunday roast with Yorkshire pudding was always the highlight of the week. You will find this recipe also in the dinner section on page 81.

I cannot remember a day when we did not have a wonderful sweet steamed pudding after dinner. It's a good thing that we had a two-hour lunch break from work!

Of course at 4:00 p.m. (afternoon tea) there was always a cup of tea and a sandwich or cake.

Farleyer House Hotel, Aberfeldy, Perthshire, Scotland

* Originally built as a croft dating back to the 16th Century, Farleyer is situated in the heart of the old Castle Menzies Estate.

Following the 1745 rebellion, when Charles Stuart was given refuge in the Castle, the croft was enlarged to become the bailiff's residence. Later on when Lady Stair married Sir Neil Menzies, Farleyer, by then the Dower House, the building was again enlarged to its present size to become the main residence for the head of the Clan Menzies.

Farleyer House became known far and wide for its own particular style of exceptional hospitality, tranquility and warmth. Today, Farleyer offers some of the most imaginative and exciting cuisine found in Britain.

* Note: a croft is a small agricultural holding rented to a Crofter who tills the land.

Phone: 011 44 1887 820 332   Fax: 011 44 1887 829 430

Crab Cakes, Guacamole Salad

From Farleyer House Hotel, Perthshire, Scotland

Crab Cakes

Serves 4 - 6
1 cup white crab meat
¾ cup diced fresh cod
⅓ cup mayonnaise
½ cup fresh breadcrumbs mixed with a little milk.
1 egg
3 tablespoons chopped chives
2 tablespoons chopped parsley
Salt, ground black pepper, and cayenne
½ cup breadcrumbs
¼ cup olive oil or canola and ¼ stick butter for frying

Combine the crab, cod, breadcrumbs in milk, and mayonnaise. Add egg and season to taste. Add the herbs. Divide into 12 pieces and shape into cakes of equal size. Dredge in the breadcrumbs and coat well.

Fry in oil and butter till crisp and brown.

Guacamole Salad

2 ripe avocados evenly chopped
½ finely chopped white onion
2 tablespoons freshly chopped coriander
2 grilled and seeded red or green chilies finely chopped.
3 diced tomatoes
Juice of one lemon or lime
Sea Salt, ground black pepper

Combine the ingredients and season to taste. Serve the crab cakes on a bed of the guacamole salad.

Pork Pie

Melton Mowbray Recipe

Melton Mowbray is a small village in Leicestershire. (A "Shire" is the British equivalent of a County in a U.S. State.) This is a robust pie from the Shires, justly famous for its juicy, jellied filling. A little anchovy essence gives the meat an extra savoury tang. The pies were originally served at high tea after a long day's hunt.

Serves 8
1 lb plain flour
1 egg yolk
6 oz lard or vegetable shortening
4 fl oz milk
2 lb lean pork, cut into ¼ inch dice
3 bacon rashers, finely diced
1 teaspoon fresh sage, finely chopped
1 teaspoon fresh thyme, finely chopped
1 teaspoon anchovy essence
½ teaspoon ground mace
½ teaspoon ground allspice
1 pint chicken stock
1 egg, beaten, to glaze
½ oz gelatin
Oven 400°F

Warm a mixing bowl and sieve the flour into it. Make a well in the center and add the egg yolk.

Gently heat the lard or shortening in the milk until it has melted, then bring rapidly to the boil. Pour immediately into the well in the flour and draw the ingredients together with a wooden spoon to form a soft, pliable but not sticky ball of dough.

Transfer to a lightly floured surface and knead until it is smooth and elastic. Cover and leave to rest in a warm place for 20-30 minutes. *(continued)*

(Melton Mowbray Pork Pie, continued)

Mix together the pork, bacon, herbs, anchovy essence and spices. Moisten with 3 tablespoons of the stock.

Roll out two thirds of the pastry on a lightly floured surface and mold round a 2½ lb floured straight sided jam jar to make a pastry cup about 2 ½ - 3 inches high, or line a raised pie mold. If using a jar, leave the pastry to set on a baking sheet, then gently ease out the jar.

Pack the meat mixture into the pastry. Roll out the remaining pastry to make a lid for the pie. Press the edges together tightly to seal. Scallop the edges and decorate with pastry leaves. Cut a hole in the centre of the lid. Tie a double thickness of buttered greaseproof paper carefully around the outside of the pie. Brush the top with beaten egg. Place on a baking sheet.

Bake for 20 minutes. Reduce the temperature to 350 °F and bake for a further 2¼ hours. Remove the mold or greaseproof paper, brush the sides and top with egg and return to the oven for 10-15 minutes, until well browned. Remove from the oven and leave until almost cold.

Heat the stock in a saucepan and sprinkle in the gelatin. Stir briskly until dissolved. Leave to cool slightly. Pour liquid through the hole in the pastry lid. Leave in a cool place overnight. Serve cut in thick slices.

Fishy Pot Pie

Serves 4
1 pound firm white fish
½ pound uncooked peeled shrimp
1 clove garlic, peeled and crushed
2 tablespoons margarine or butter
2 tablespoons olive oil
1 tablespoon chopped parsley
2 teaspoons Dijon mustard
1 large potato, par boiled and diced small
1 cup peas
½ cup white wine
½ cup 100% cream
1 tablespoon fresh lemon juice
2 tablespoons cornstarch
¼ teaspoon each salt and pepper

Topping:
2 cups fresh breadcrumbs
1 cup parmesan cheese
Oven 400°F

Cut the fish fillets into 1" strips and the shrimps in half. Peel and crush the garlic. Mix cornstarch with a little of the wine, mustard and seasonings. Mix breadcrumbs with the Parmesan.

Put the butter and oil in skillet and sauté the garlic. Add the fish then wine, lemon juice and peas. Stir well before adding the cornstarch mix and parsley. Stir again and add the cream.

Pour into individual ovenproof dishes. Divide the breadcrumb mixture equally between the four servings and sprinkle on the top. Cook for 8-10 minutes until topping is light brown.

Serve hot with a side dish of watercress and tomatoes on butter lettuce.

Picnic Chicken and Nut Loaf

1 whole chicken, medium size
2 cups water
¼ teaspoon salt
¼ teaspoon pepper
½ teaspoon paprika
½ cup slivered almonds
¼ cup soft breadcrumbs
2 eggs
Oven 350°F

Make Chicken Stock:
Boil the chicken in a large pot of water for about 40 minutes.
Remove the chicken from the water. When cooled, strip the
meat from the bones. Return the bones with the giblets to the
water and simmer with the seasonings for one hour.

Strain the giblets and bones from the stock, and discard the
bones.

Finely chop or mince the chicken and giblets and combine them.
Add the nuts, breadcrumbs, eggs and ¼ pint of the chicken
stock. Season again and put in a well-greased 2-pound loaf pan,
or mold. Cover with foil. Bake for 1½ hours. Refrigerate for at
least three hours before serving.

Turn out onto a bed of lettuce. Slice, and serve with cheese and
brown bread and butter. The loaf also makes a good filling for
sandwiches.

Crusted Goat's Cheese Salad

From Chef Christopher Gilber,
Milford Hall Hotel, Salisbury, Wiltshire

Serves 2
2 slices goat's cheese, 1 inch thick
4 slices dry breadcrumbs
¼ cup chopped walnuts
1 egg, beaten
½ cup flour
1 cup olive oil
2 cups mixed salad greens

Dressing
1 inch fresh root ginger, grated
1 red chili, finely diced
1 clove finely chopped garlic
Zest of 1 lime
1 cup white wine vinegar
2/3 cup sugar

Dressing:
Place all the ingredients in a pan and bring to the boil, then reduce the heat and simmer for 10 minutes – leave to cool

For the Salad:
Mix the breadcrumbs and walnuts together. Coat each slice of goat's cheese with flour, egg and breadcrumbs and set aside in the fridge for ½ - 1 hour.

Heat olive oil in heavy-bottomed frying pan on medium heat. When hot, add goat's cheese and fry for about 3 minutes. Drain well with paper towel.

Arrange mixed salad leaves on plate with the goat's cheese on top. Drizzle with the sweet chili dressing.

Bishopstrow House, Warminster, Wiltshire

Bishopstrow House is a charming Georgian country house built in 1817, surrounded by acres of beautiful English gardens through which runs the River Wylye, great for trout fishing. Close by are heritage sites of the Roman city of Bath and one of Britain's most extraordinary landmarks, the 4000 year-old monument of Stonehenge. The hotel's interior reveals many fine rooms with graceful features and elegant proportions. Roaring log fires, antiques and fresh flowers enhance the dramatic décor.

Chef Steve Bywater cooks modern British cuisine with a dedication to fresh West Country produce. The house features both indoor and outdoor tennis courts and heated swimming pools, hair studio and beauty treatments at the Ragdale Spa by Michaeljohn of London and Beverly Hills. Trap shooting and archery are available in the grounds.

Location: Bishopstrow House is located in the country outside the town centre of Warminster, surrounded by acres of beautiful English gardens and by the River Wylye, close to Bath and Stonehenge, two hours from London.

Phone: 011 44 1985 212312   Fax: 011-44-1985-216769

Fish en Croûte

Serves 4
1 packet frozen puff pastry
1 oz butter,
1 teaspoon olive oil
½ lb cod fillet or other firm fish
Salt and pepper
Juice of ½ lemon
1 tablespoon chopped parsley
1 egg
4 sprigs parsley
Oven 450°F

Roll out the pastry very thinly. Cut out four 3-inch squares, place on a cookie sheet and refrigerate while making the filling.

Melt the butter and oil in a pan, skin the fish and cut into small pieces. Add to the pan with salt, pepper, lemon juice and parsley. Mix well, cover and cook for 5 minutes, shaking the pan often.

Beat the egg, add half to the fish and mix well. Divide the mixture between the pastries, keeping it well in the center.

Dampen the edges of the pastry with water and bring the four corners to the center, pressing well to seal. Brush with the remaining egg. Bake on the top shelf of the preheated oven for 10 minutes, or until golden brown.

Garnish with the parsley and serve with a green salad or vegetables of your choice.

Ploughman's Lunch

Although no cooking is required for this lunch, I feel it should be mentioned because it is ubiquitous on pub-grub menus.

Ploughman's Lunch consists of cheese, thick cut crusty bread and butter, chutney and or pickled onions.

Usually three or four different types of cheese are cut into wedges. Cheddar, Brie or Camembert and Stilton are popular. A soft(ish) cheese is normally included with two firmer ones.

This is best served in a sunny pub garden with a glass of dry sherry or a shandy. (Shandy is half and half light beer and English lemonade, which is the same as American Seven-Up or Sprite).

There is a chutney available in this country imported from U.K. called Branston Pickle. It is a perfect accompaniment with this lunch, as is the Beetroot Chutney on the following page.

About Cheese
Cheese is mentioned in the Old Testament and was one of the first manufactured foods. Cheese is made from the concentrated curd of milk; the curd can be formed through the action of the rennet or by means of lactic acid.

Cheeses come into two basic types, hard and soft. The difference between them rests on the amount of moisture (called whey) left in the curd, the bacteria or mold used to produce their distinctive flavor and the method of curing.

The most popular cheese in America is surely Cheddar. Few people realize that this fine cheese originated in England in Cheddar Gorge, in the south- west of England. Today Cheddar is produced in most parts of the world.

Many cheeses can be bought here that originated in England and are named after the towns where they were, and still are, made

Beetroot Chutney

Excellent served with cold cuts of meat and cheeses

>*3 pounds beets (Beetroot in England)*
>*2 medium size cooking apples peeled and cored*
>*2 large onions*
>*1 cup sugar*
>*½ pint malt vinegar*
>*1 teaspoons salt*
>*1 teaspoon pepper*

Boil beets until tender. Set aside to cool. Peel beets and chop up small. Chop onions finely. Dice apples into small pieces.

In a large pan, add sugar, vinegar, seasoning and chopped onion. Cook until onion is transparent and apples are soft. Add beetroot last and cook over medium heat until mixture thickens.

Pour into sterile hot jars and seal. Store in a cool place.

Macaroni Egg Pie

Serves 4
1 cup elbow macaroni, cooked
2 large eggs
½ pint milk
1 cup grated cheese
¼ chopped chives
2 cups broccoli, cooked, cut small
8 inch casserole dish
Oven 300°F

Grease the dish and spread out the cooked macaroni in it. Add the broccoli and chives. Beat the eggs and milk together and add half the cheese. Pour this over the broccoli and sprinkle the remaining cheese on top.

Bake in the oven until it is set. Serve with a green salad.

This delicious dish can be made with any vegetables you choose or with onions.

The Horn of Plenty, Gulworthy, Tavistock, Devon

The house was built in 1830 for a mine captain at the Devon Consul mines. In the last century the Tamar valley was full of tin mines, the Devon Consol being one of the largest.

The house was bought in the late sixties by Patrick and Sonia Stevenson and turned into a restaurant, which became famous under the guidance of Sonia, a truly talented chef.

In the early eighties six new bedrooms were added in the old coach house, which overlooks the valley, bringing the total number of bedrooms to ten.

In 1990 Elaine and Ian Gatehouse bought the 'Horn' and brought with them Peter Gorton to be the chef. In 1999 Peter, with his business partner Paul Roston bought the 'Horn' and are keeping up the fine tradition of good food and hospitality.

(continued)

(The Horn of Plenty – history, continued.)

The Horn of Plenty is one of those very special places that one constantly seeks but rarely finds. The property nestles into the Tamar valley surrounded by 4 acres of gardens and orchard; the gardens are ablaze with camellias, azaleas and rhododendrons from early spring to mid summer. Inside the house there is an immediacy of warmth and welcome and the smell of fresh flowers competing with the tang of wood smoke from the log fires in winter.

The heart of The Horn of Plenty is the kitchen, and they take their cooking very seriously. Peter Gorton is a Michelin Star Chef whose dishes are full of flavors, texture, harmony and contrast, balance and of course, the final presentation. All of these are of course as important as the fresh produce and top quality ingredients that combine to make a memorable meal.

Phone: 011-44-1822-832528   Fax: 011-44-1822-832528

Baked Goat's Cheese Parcels with Sweet and Sour Leeks

from Chef Peter Gorton, The Horn of Plenty, Tavistock, Devon

Serves 4
Goat's cheese in filo:
2 oz roughly chopped hazelnuts & pistachios
½ lb/1 pack (8 sheets) filo pastry
6 oz goat's cheese
2oz butter
Oven 400°F

Mix the goat's cheese with salt and pepper to taste, shape the cheese into 12 small balls. Set aside.

Place 1 sheet of filo on a flat surface and brush with butter. Sprinkle over the chopped hazelnuts and pistachios, season and press another sheet of filo on top then butter and season it. Place 3 pieces of goat's cheese on the pastry and cut a round shape around the cheese to form little money bag shapes (3 in diameter circles). Repeat until you have 12 parcels in all. Place in the fridge to firm - (5 min). Place on a baking sheet and bake for 8 - 10 minutes or until golden brown.

Beetroot Dressing:
2 teaspoons Dijon mustard
3 tablespoons red wine vinegar
3 tablespoons of water
½ teaspoon sugar
1 clove garlic, peeled and quartered
¼ teaspoon freshly ground pepper to taste
3 tablespoons olive oil
A selection of chopped fresh herbs
6oz finely chopped, cooked or vacuum packed beetroots

In a blender combine mustard, vinegar, water, sugar, garlic and pepper. Process until blended; stir in beetroot and chopped fresh herbs.

(continued)

(Baked Goat's Cheese Parcels with Sweet and Sour Leeks continued.)

Sweet and sour Leeks:
>2¼ lb leeks
>2 cloves of garlic
>1 tablespoon sugar
>4 tablespoons olive oil
>Juice of 1 lemon
>1 Tablespoon soy sauce (optional)

Clean the leeks thoroughly. Cut off the tough green part. Cut the leeks into longish slices. Fry the crushed garlic and sugar in hot oil until the sugar caramelizes slightly. Add the leeks and turn them a little over moderate heat. Sprinkle with lemon juice. Cover and stew gently over a low heat until tender. Serve hot or cold.

Tomato Garnish:
>1 medium tomato
>2 tbsp olive oil
>2 tsp fresh mixed herbs

To Assemble
Place a small mound of the leaks in the middle of each plate and place a goat's cheese parcel on top. Spoon round the beetroot dressing and decorate each plate with the tomato garnish.

Cornish Pasties

(pronounced "pastees")

Cornish pasties originated about 800 years ago as lunches for tin miners, fishermen and farmers to take to work. Housewives used to make one for each member of the household and mark their initials on the crust of each pastie. The miners carried their pasties to work in a tin bucket, which they heated by burning a candle underneath.

Traditionally, pasties are a complete meal, their contents varying slightly in different parts of the country. The traditional way of eating the pasty is in the hand, which was convenient for the tin miners who sometimes had to work waist-deep in water, the only light being from the candles fixed to their tin hats.

Makes 4 pasties

Pastry:
¾ cup lard or vegetable shortening
¾ cup water
2 cups flour w/pinch salt
1 egg w/little milk for top of pastry

Combine the flour and salt in a large bowl. Using pastry blender, cut shortening into flour. Make a well in the center of mixture and quickly stir in ice cold water. Form dough into a ball. Set aside.

Roll out the pastry dough to approximately ¼ inch, and use an 8 inch plate and knife to cut pastry rounds.

(continued)

(Cornish Pasties continued)

Filling:
½ *pound top sirloin, diced small*
1 *medium potato, diced*
1 *carrot, chopped finely*
½ *cup peas*
1 *clove garlic, crushed*
1 *medium onion diced small*
1 *teaspoon salt*
½ *teaspoon pepper*
½ *teaspoon thyme*
1 *cup water with a little gravy browning*
1 *tablespoon flour mixed to paste with water*
2 *tablespoons oil*
Oven 400°F

Slice and dice the vegetables and meat. Make the gravy with gravy browning, flour and water. Set aside.

Sauté garlic and onion in the oil until soft. Push to edge of skillet. Brown the meat on high heat. Lower heat and add seasonings. Cook, stirring until meat is tender, about 5 minutes. Add gravy mix, stirring until thick. Add peas, potato and carrots. Cook on low heat covered, while making the pastry - about 7 minutes. Mixture should be very moist.

Put ¾ cup of the meat mixture into the pastry round, fold up the two edges to seal securely like a pouch. Prick top of pastry with a fork and brush with beaten egg and milk.

Bake on cookie sheet, 30 minutes until pastry is golden.

Pasties can be eaten hot with a little extra gravy and vegetables, or cold as a picnic snack.

Beef and Ham Pâté Loaf

1½ pound top round steak
12 ounce calf's or beef liver
1 pound cooked ham
¼ cup margarine
1 tablespoon flour and 1 beef bouillon cube dissolved in
½ cup of hot water
1 cup milk
5 tablespoons thick cream
3 tablespoons dry sherry
5 eggs (2 beaten, 3 hard boiled)
2 teaspoons fresh chopped marjoram
¼ teaspoon salt
½ teaspoon pepper
Oven 325°F

Chop steak, liver and ham very finely. In saucepan, melt margarine, add flour and stir well for a few minutes, then add the beef liquid and milk. Stir until thick. Add the cream, sherry, 2 beaten eggs, marjoram, salt and pepper. Add all the meats and blend well.

Shell the hard-boiled eggs. Put half of the meat mixture into a greased 4-pint loaf pan. Arrange whole eggs lengthwise on top. Cover with remaining meat mixture. Cover with foil or wax paper.

Stand in a pan of cold water and bake for 1½ hours in center of oven. Cool in pan. Turn out just before serving on to large plate. Since this loaf is rather rich, it is usually served in ½ inch slices. Garnish with black olives, red and green peppers, and serve on a lettuce leaf.

Crusty bread and butter go well with this dish.

Welsh Rarebit

3 cups grated cheddar cheese
¼ cup butter
1 egg
2 tablespoons beer or milk
1 tablespoon Dijon mustard
4 slices bread
Oven on broil

Blend the cheese with the mustard, egg, beer (or milk) and half of the butter. Toast the bread and spread with remaining butter and the cheese mixture. Place on a cookie sheet and broil for about 4 minutes.

To vary, put a slice of ham on the toast before the cheese mixture. Also, a poached egg on top of each serving gives a more robust meal.

The Old Rectory, Willersey, Gloucestershire

There are hundreds of ancient and Beautiful Cotswold villages dotted and nestled throughout this most unique and beautiful area of England. The village of Willersey is located 1 mile North East of the better-known village of Broadway. Willersey's manor house was home to the Roper family, William Roper becoming son in-law to Sir Thomas More.

The Old Rectory is a 17th century country house at its best with its superb decoration and tasteful furnishings. Built in mellow Cotswold stone, it retains all of its original oak beams and quaint old fireplaces. The original charm has been lovingly maintained.

The Old Rectory is located in a quiet cul-de-sac, edged with colorful cottages and an ancient 11th Century church.

Phone/Fax: 011 44 386 853729

Busy Lizzie's Seafood Salad

from The Old Rectory, Willersey, Gloucestershire

Serves 4
1 cup crab meat, large chunks
1 cup of shrimp or lobster or a mixture of both
1 medium sized cucumber
1 small cantaloupe melon

Vinaigrette Dressing
½ teaspoon salt
1 teaspoon sugar
1 teaspoon dry mustard
3 tablespoons white wine vinegar
½ cup olive oil
1 tablespoon of chopped mint

Cut the melon and cucumber into bite size pieces. Add to the seafood.

Mix all the dressing ingredients in a separate container.

Coat the fish, melon & cucumber with the dressing and leave in fridge for a few hours.

Add your favorite green salad mix and toss lightly.

Serve with hot crusty bread.

Potted Shrimp

1 pound cooked peeled small shrimp
¼ cup (plus one tablespoon) butter
¼ teaspoon black pepper
1 teaspoon nutmeg
1 pinch cayenne pepper
1 pinch salt
Juice of one lemon
Oven 350°F

In medium saucepan, melt the ¼ cup butter over low heat to clarify. Grease four individual 4-ounce ovenproof (ramekin) dishes.

In separate bowl pour lemon juice over the shrimp and coat thoroughly. Add salt, cayenne, nutmeg, and black pepper; stir lightly. Pack shrimp into the individual pots. Dot each with a little butter and bake for 10 minutes. Cool.

Pour the clarified butter over shrimp and refrigerate over night.

Turn each pot out on to a lettuce leaf. Serve with brown bread and butter or toast points (very thinly sliced toast, cut diagonally) and wedge of lemon.

Ramekins:
Ramekins are small round or oval bowls, not unlike custard cups, usually fluted and white. They are available in many sizes with high sides for meat pies, low sides for flan dishes and Crème Brûlée. The 6 ounce ramekins are good for potted shrimp, sauces, dips, etc.

ENGLISH TEA

At one time workplaces closed down for a tea break at
4:0p.m. I doubt this happens any longer! Afternoon tea
is normally served on Sundays around 4:00 o'clock
although teashops throughout Britain serve tea at almost
any time of the day.

High tea is a far more sumptuous affair. If you are
invited to high tea you can usually expect assorted
sandwiches, sherry trifle and cake or cakes with tea
served in china cups. Two of the favorite sandwiches
served at tea are English cucumber (which are sweeter
with smaller, softer and less bitter seeds,) and egg and
watercress.

The Empress Hotel in Victoria, B. C., Canada, often
serves English Crumpets with high tea so to give you
the chance to make and sample them I've included the
recipe for crumpets from Hartwell House in this section.

How to make a "Proper" cup of tea.

1. Fill the kettle with fresh, cold, water. Do not use the water that is sitting in the kettle as it has already been boiled and de-oxygenated.

2. Bring the water to a rapid boil.

3. Pour a little water from the kettle into the teapot, swirl it around and then pour it away. (This is known as "warming the pot.")

4. Put one generous teaspoon of tea per person in the teapot plus one additional spoonful ("one for the pot").

5. Pour the boiling water into the teapot and stir.

6. Replace the lid on the teapot and allow the tea to brew (set, steep, mash, etc.) for 5 minutes before serving.

7. Refill the kettle with more water and bring it to a boil so that you will have water on hand to replenish the teapot when necessary.

8. There is an age-old controversy as to whether the milk should be poured into the cup before (ante-lacteal) or after (post-lacteal) the tea. Regardless of which way you choose to do it, be sure that the milk is cold and that it really is milk and not cream.

9. Always use a tea strainer when using loose tea (or if you absolutely must, you can cheat by using tea-bags).

Different blends of tea:

ASSAM: *A heavy, pungent tea from Northern India that is used in many blends.*

CEYLON: *Strong and dark.*

DARJEELING: *A delicate, amber-colored tea that is grown in the foothills of the Himalayas.*

EARL GREY: *A blend of Darjeeling and China tea that is scented with spices. It is a light and delicate tea good for afternoon tea.*

ENGLISH BREAKFAST: *A rich blend of China and Indian tea.*

LAPSANG SOUCHONG: *A China tea that has a smoky flavor and comes mainly from Taiwan.*

RUSSIAN: *A blend of Chinese teas with a good, robust flavor.*

AMERICAN BLACK: *A cover-all name for all the lesser grades of tea that are used in tea bags and tend to be somewhat bland and uninteresting.*

Cucumber Sandwiches

English cucumber (Canadian, hothouse grown) sliced thinly
White bread, traditionally very fresh and thinly sliced
Cream cheese
¾ cup English style Malt vinegar
2 tablespoons sugar
¾ water

Place the sliced cucumber in a bowl with the malt vinegar, water and sugar and leave for ½ hour. (Don't let cucumber turn brown.)

Spread each slice of bread lightly with cream cheese. Put 4 rounds of cucumber on one piece of bread and top with another.

When there is a stack of sandwiches, carefully cut off all the crusts. Cut each sandwich into 4 so that each small sandwich has a round of cucumber in it.

Egg and Cress Sandwiches

3 hard-boiled eggs
Watercress
2 tablespoons mayonnaise
6 slices of brown (wheat) buttered bread
Salt & pepper

Peel and mash eggs, and mix with mayonnaise. Spread the buttered bread with the egg mixture and add generous sprigs of watercress. Sprinkle with salt & pepper.

Make sandwiches and slice each in half or diagonally. The crusts may be removed or not at your discretion.

Stack sandwiches on paper doilies on pretty china plates.

Vodka Grapefruit Mousse

from Chef Christopher Gilber,
Milford Hall Hotel, Salisbury, Wiltshire

Christopher's Favorite Dessert

> *Serves 6*
> *4 tablespoons vodka*
> *1 sachet of powdered gelatin*
> *1 grapefruit*
> *3 large eggs – separated*
> *¾ cup sugar*
> *3 tablespoons lime juice*
> *1 cup double cream*

Pour the vodka into a small bowl and sprinkle over the gelatin. Place the small bowl inside a larger one half filled with hot water to heat the bowl of vodka gelatin gently. Set aside.

Finely grate the zest of the grapefruit and place it in a large mixing bowl with the egg yolks and ½ a cup of the sugar. Whisk with a electric whisk until the mixture is pale and thick. Stir the gelatin to ensure that it has fully dissolved.

Squeeze the juice from the grapefruit and mix it into the gelatin before stirring the mixture into the beaten egg yolks with the limejuice.

Put the mixture into the fridge, stirring regularly until it begins to thicken and set. This takes about 15 minutes.

Whip the cream until it holds soft floppy peaks. Using a metal spoon, gently fold the cream into the grapefruit gelatin mixture. When the mixture is holding its shape, whisk the egg yolks until they form soft peaks, then whisk in the remaining ¼ cup of sugar. Fold the egg yolks into the mousse and spoon into 6 individual dishes. Chill until needed.

Hartwell House, Aylesbury, Buckinghamshire

Hartwell House has a remarkable history, stretching back almost a thousand years to the reign of Edward the Confessor. This house was mentioned in the Domesday Book (1068 AD) as the property of William Peveral the natural son of William the Conqueror. Richard the Lion Heart, who was King of England in 1199, lived there and Louis XVIII, the exiled King of France held court there from 1809 to 1814.

Many English dignitaries and royalty occupied Hartwell until travel tycoon Thomas Cook purchased the house. Hartwell House served as an Army billet during the Second World War and as a training ground for British and American troops.

As with most historic homes the architecture of Hartwell House has changed over the centuries. Each owner left his mark with additions and changes, though parts of the house remain unchanged such as the chapel, the Jacobean staircase, and the observatory. Hartwell has thirty-one bedrooms and suites on two floors as well as a health and beauty spa.

Phone: 011 44 296 747444   Fax: 011 44 296 747450

Traditional English Crumpets

from Hartwell House, Aylesbury, Buckinghamshire

5 cups all purpose flour
1 teaspoon cream of tartar
¾ teaspoon sugar
¾ ounce yeast
1 pint water

½ teaspoon bicarbonate of soda
1 ½ teaspoon salt
5 fl ounce water

Beat the first 5 ingredients together well to make a batter and let stand for 45 minutes, then beat in the bicarbonate of soda, salt and water.

Lightly grease the crumpet hoops (egg rings). Pour the batter into the hoops on the hotplate using a ladle. When the crumpets have fully 'holed', turn them over so that they can brown very slightly. This takes away the raw appearance and makes them more attractive.

If the hoops are too heavily greased, the butter will run on the hotplate and the resultant crumpets will be 'blind', that is, they will not show the characteristic network of holes. The hotplate must be burnished and absolutely free from grease.

Crumpets are wonderful for breakfast with butter, honey or jam, or equally pleasing for afternoon tea.

Sherry Trifle

It wasn't until the 18th Century that sweetened fruit jelly (Jello) was available to the masses, coinciding with the reduction in the price of sugar. It is not known who first came up with the idea of combining jelly with cake soaked in sherry or fruit juice, custard and cream, but the resulting dessert is delicious.

10 Lady Fingers or 18" sponge layer	**Custard:**
1/3 cup raspberry jam	*1/2 pint milk*
3/4 cup sherry	*1/4 cup sugar*
1/2 pint real cream	*2 eggs (separate yolk*
1/4 cup sliced almonds lightly toasted	*from whites)*
8 maraschino cherries chopped	
2 tablespoons juice from cherry bottle	

Spread each ladyfinger or each piece of sponge cake with raspberry jam. Line the bottom of a large glass bowl with the cake or ladyfingers with the jam side up.

Pour sherry over the top. Let it soak for a few minutes before adding the halved cherries and juice.

Custard:
Blend egg yolks and sugar in a bowl. Warm the milk and pour it over the egg mixture. Stir well and return to the pan to thicken over low heat. Pour over the sponge and leave to set. Do not refrigerate.

Just before serving, whip the cream with the egg whites into peaks and pour over the dish. Decorate with almonds.

There's an imported custard mix called "Birds Dessert Powder" which is available in some stores or you can buy a package of vanilla pudding for the custard layer. If you are making the trifle a day or two before serving, refrigerate but let it stand for an hour or two before adding cream so that the sherry flavor comes through.

Angela's Sherry Trifle, Quick Version

1 packet of Lady Fingers if available or Angel Food Cake
1 pint milk
1 packet Bird's Dessert Mix to make the custard
2 tablespoons sugar
1 packet of Jello, any red fruit flavor
1 15 oz can Blackberries
½ cup Sherry
1 pint (20 fl oz) double or whipped cream
Maraschino Cherries to decorate
Blackberry Preserve (Jam)

Spread the jam on the lady Fingers or 1" thick pieces of Angel Food Cake. Place the pieces of sponge cake in a pretty 3½ pint glass bowl and soak with the sherry.

Strain the juice from the can of blackberries and set aside. Spread the blackberries evenly over the cake and sherry.

Make the Jello as instructions on the packet and top with fruit juice from the blackberries to make a pint. Pour over the soaked cakes and leave to set overnight.

Make the custard with the Bird's Dessert Mix, milk and sugar (follow the directions on the packet). Remove from the heat and leave until cool. Remove the skin which will have formed on the custard and pour the custard on top of the jello, fruit etc. Refrigerate until just before serving.

Whip the cream or make the topping and spoon carefully over the trifle.

Decorate with glace cherries, chill and serve.

Caraway Scones

1 pound of flour
1 teaspoon baking powder
1 teaspoon baking soda dissolved in
1 teaspoon water
½ cup butter or margarine
¾ cup sugar
2 tablespoons caraway seeds
2 tablespoons marmalade
1 tablespoon vinegar
½ cup buttermilk
Oven 400°F

In a large bowl, mix flour, baking powder and shortening (margarine or butter). Rub together and crumble until fine. Add sugar and caraway seeds and mix. Make a well in the middle and add marmalade, baking soda and vinegar.

Mix to a stiff dough with the buttermilk. Roll out to ½ inch and cut into rounds with cookie cutter. Bake until light brown on cookie sheet for 20 minutes. Makes 12 scones.

Scones, pronounced "sconz", originated in Scotland and can be made without the caraway seeds as plain scones, or with golden raisins, (which in England are known as sultanas).

Eccles Cakes

Eccles is a town near Manchester in the north of England.

Pastry:
1½ cups flour
7 tablespoons unsalted butter
2 tablespoons vegetable shortening
1 tablespoon sugar
¼ teaspoon salt
3-5 tablespoons ice water

Filling:
¼ cup butter
1 cup currants
¼ cup sugar
¼ cup candied peel
1 teaspoon nutmeg
Oven 425°F

Make Pastry:
Cut the butter and shortening into pieces. In a large bowl, combine the shortening and dry ingredients. Blend together until the mixture feels like course breadcrumbs. Add ice water as necessary to make the dough pliable. Form into a ball, wrap in wax paper and chill for one hour.

Filling:
Mix all of the ingredients together in a bowl and put in the refrigerator with the pastry for the remainder of the hour.

Roll out and cut the pastry into rounds with a 3-inch cookie cutter. Put a teaspoon of the cold filling mixture on each round. Wet the edges and fold the round to draw the edges together. Turn over and roll out until the currants show through.

Make a few cuts on top with a knife and bake for 20 minutes.

Ginger Bread

2 cups flour
½ cup butter
½ cup vegetable shortening
1 cup brown sugar
2 teaspoons ground ginger
¼ teaspoon nutmeg
¼ cup grated lemon peel
2 eggs beaten
1 teaspoon baking soda dissolved in
2 teaspoons warm milk
Oven 325°F

Cut the shortening into pieces on a cutting board. Mix the flour and spices (ginger and nutmeg) together in a large bowl. Add the shortening to the flour and rub together to make a course meal consistency. Mix in the lemon peel and sugar. Add eggs and mix to make a stiff paste.

Dissolve the soda in the warm milk and mix in the mixture.

Pour into a 7-8 inch square cake pan lined with wax paper.

Bake for one hour, or until the bread starts to pull away from the edges of the pan.

Shortbread

2 cups flour
1 cup butter (2 sticks)
½ cup fine granulated sugar
Oven 300°F

Cream the butter and sugar until fluffy. Gradually fold in the flour until it is like soft dough. The recipe is enough for two 8-inch shallow pie plates.

Divide the dough and press into the pie plates. Make a fancy edging around the edge with a spoon handle or knife. Score, (make light cuts) from the center to divide into 8 or 10 pieces.

Bake for 30 minutes on the top oven shelf, or until golden brown. Shortbread should be crisp, not doughy when done.

Coconut Pyramids

4 egg whites
½ cup sugar
½ cup flaked coconut
rice paper optional
4 drops each pink and green coloring
Oven 350° F

Whisk egg whites till stiff and fold in the sugar and coconut. Divide mixture into two and add pink to one mix and green to the other. Mold into four pyramids of each color.

Bake on a greased cookie sheet ... or cookie sheet lined with rice paper for 30 - 40 minutes until slightly browned.

Rock Cakes

2 cups flour
2 teaspoons baking powder
½ teaspoon salt
½ cup butter
½ cup sugar
1 cup mixed dried fruit
¼ teaspoon nutmeg
1 egg
1/3 cup milk
Oven 350°F

Sieve the flour, salt and baking powder together. Rub the butter into the flour until the mixture resembles fine breadcrumbs. Stir in the sugar, fruit and nutmeg.

Beat the egg with the milk and add to the flour mixture. Mix well with a fork; the mixture should be stiff but not too sticky and should leave the sides of the mixing bowl clean.

Divide the mixture into 12 and place on a greased tray; rough up with a fork. Bake in a moderately hot oven for 15 to 20 minutes. Cool on a wire tray.

Rock cakes are not rich and are therefore best eaten on the day they are baked. For a crunchy topping, sprinkle with sugar before baking.

Castleton Vicarage Cake

Castleton is a small village on the Yorkshire Moors in the north of England. The vicar's wife made her special cakes to sell at the local village pub to raise money for the church: hence the name Castleton Vicarage Cake.

4 cups all-purpose flour
1 1/2 cups brown sugar
1 cup currants
1 cup golden raisins
½ cup candied peel
12 ounces real butter (3 sticks)
pinch of salt if butter is unsalted
1 teaspoon baking soda
¼ cup milk
Oven 350ºF

Grease and lightly flour an 8-inch round cake pan. Mix flour, sugar, fruit, candied peel and baking soda together in a large bowl. Make a well in center. Cut the butter into small pieces and add to middle of bowl. Boil the milk and pour over the butter. Mix well.

Pour into pan & bake for 2 hours until cake starts to pull away from sides of pan or test for doneness with a wooden toothpick.

This cake can be stored in an airtight container and will last for weeks.

Victoria Sponge

4 ounce butter
3 eggs
1 tablespoon milk
2/3 cup sugar
1 cup flour
1 teaspoon baking powder
Salt
Confectioner's Sugar (powdered sugar)
Oven 375°F

Filling
Strawberry jam
1 cup heavy cream

Melt the butter in a saucepan over very low heat, making sure it does not boil.

Make sure the eggs and milk are at room temperature and beat together. Add sugar and beat well.

In a separate bowl sift the flour, baking powder and a pinch of salt. Fold gently into the egg mixture. Stir in the melted butter.

Divide the mixture between 2 well-greased 7-inch cake pans and bake side by side for 12 to 15 minutes or until golden and well risen.

Remove from the oven and cool for at least 10 minutes before turning the cake onto a cake rack.

Fill the two sandwiches with jam or with whipped cream and jam.

This sponge is perfect for sherry trifle.

HORS D'OEUVRES AND STARTERS

The British are a little more reserved than Americans in their choice of hors d'oeuvres or appetizers for cocktail parties. Assorted nuts and canapés are usual fare and at holiday times there may be Scotch Eggs and Sausage Rolls, see pages 73 and 74 respectively.

However, substantial starters usually make up for the lack of appetizers. At good restaurants you will often find a fish course on the menu followed by fruit (grapefruit or melon) or soup, with a fruit sorbet to cleanse the palette before the main course.

I love to serve an interesting salad or soup and have included some wonderful recipes from the chefs from historic hotels and pubs in Britain.

Coq a Leekie Soup

Sir Walter Scott often mentioned this soup in his famous diaries. The prunes add a different but delicious taste.

Serves 4
4 small chicken breasts
4 washed and trimmed leeks cut into 1 inch pieces
½ cup rice
1 tablespoon salt
1 lb pitted prunes
½ cup chopped parsley

In a large saucepan with approximately 3 pints water, boil chicken breast for 15 minutes until just cooked. When the chicken has cooled cut into bite size chunks. Put back into the water with the leeks, rice and salt. Simmer gently for 2 hours.

Add prunes and continue to simmer for another ½ hour.

Season to taste and add parsley just before serving.

Summer Potato Leek Soup

Serves 4
2 large potatoes, peeled and chopped
3 large leeks, washed thoroughly and chopped
2 cups chicken stock or water
2 chicken flavor bouillon cubes
¼ pound button mushrooms, sliced
1 cup 'half and half' cream
¼ teaspoon salt
¼ teaspoon pepper
¼ cup chopped chives for garnish

Simmer the potatoes and leeks in the chicken stock for 40 minutes. Add mushrooms. Emulsify in blender. Let cool and blend with cream and seasoning.

Serve cold and sprinkle with chopped chives.

Milebrook House, Knighton, Powys, Wales

Milebrook House is situated in the beautiful Teme valley amongst the wooded, rolling Marches landscape, with the mountains and moorlands of Wales to the west. This charming house dates from 1756 and was once the home of the explorer and author Sir Wilfred Thesiger, and the one-time retreat of Haile Selassie, Emperor of Ethiopia.

The house, which is set amongst three acres of grounds, has been sensitively restored and adapted to the needs of a country house hotel. There are ten spacious bedrooms, all with en-suite bathrooms, a residents' sitting room, a lounge bar and an attractive restaurant in which lunch and dinner are available.

The hotel has a traditional style, concentrating on informal comfort, attentive but unobtrusive service and fresh, mainly homegrown ingredients cooked with imagination.

Phone: 011 44 1547 528632   Fax: 011 44 1547 520509

Beetroot and Tomato Soup

from Milebrook House, Knighton, Powys, Wales

Serves 4
1 onion, peeled and finely chopped
1 small carrot, peeled and finely chopped
1 celery stalk, trimmed and chopped
¼ cup olive oil
3 cloves of garlic peeled and crushed
2 tablespoons chopped fresh dill or dill seed
1-15 ounce can peeled whole tomatoes
2 cups cooked beets
4 cups chicken stock

Cook the onion, celery and carrot in a heavy saucepan, in the olive oil for 20 – 30 minutes without browning.

Add garlic and dill and cook for 2 – 3 minutes.

Add tomatoes, cook on high heat until much of the juice has evaporated.

Stir in the beets and stock and bring to the boil. Simmer for 15 minutes. Rub through a sieve into a clean saucepan and bring to the boil.

Serve immediately. Spoon a little cream into each soup bowl if you like and garnish with fronds of fresh dill.

The Kings Arms, Old Amersham, Buckinghamshire

The Kings Arms is a fine restaurant in the centre of Old Amersham. It was used as "The Lucky Boatman" in the film "Four Weddings and a Funeral".

This hostelry is one of England's oldest pubs, and consisted originally of two separate timber-framed open-halled houses, both built about 1450, either side of the covered entrances to the inn yard. These separate buildings formed the original Kings Arms before 1822. Both houses were modernized in the mid sixteenth century by the addition of large central brick chimney with back-to-back open hearths. Two of these have four-centered arches giving a date of c. 1550. Both houses were extended backwards in the eighteenth century and the left side house was given a Georgian front with sash windows.

Benskins brewery acquired both properties in 1934 and the whole building was extensively restored in 1936. John Jennison took over in 1977 acquired the freehold in 1993 and is still busy extensively restoring it.

Phone: 011 44 1494 726333   Fax: 011 44 1494 433480

Cucumber and Cheese Mousse

from The King's Arms, Old Amersham, Buckinghamshire

Serves 4
1 large English (Canadian) cucumber,(hothouse grown)
¼ pint boiling water
6 ounce cream cheese
2 tablespoons white wine vinegar
1 teaspoon juice from onion
salt and pepper
1 tablespoon sugar
¼ cup gelatin
1 pinch mace
3 tablespoons cold water
¼ pint double cream, lightly whipped

Dice cucumber finely, sprinkle with salt and leave pressed between two plates for half an hour.

Beat the cream cheese with the onion juice and season. Soak the gelatin in cold water, pour on the boiling water and stir until dissolved. Mix into the cheese.

Drain the cucumber thoroughly and mix with the vinegar, sugar and mace. When the cheese mixture is cool, fold in the cucumber and cream. Turn into a greased mold or into ramekin dishes (custard cups) and chill until set.

Scotch Eggs

These can be served in place of deviled eggs with before-dinner drinks.

> *4 large eggs hard boiled and shelled*
> *1 pound sausage meat*
> *1 cup breadcrumbs or crushed cornflakes*
> *1 teaspoon seasoned salt*
> *1 teaspoon dill weed.*
> *1 egg, beaten with a little milk*

Cover sausage meat with sheet of wax paper and roll out until ¼ inch thick.

Mix breadcrumbs with seasoning. Wrap each egg with the sausage meat. It helps to keep hands wet when molding the sausage meat around the eggs.

Brush with beaten egg mixture. Roll the covered eggs in the breadcrumbs.

Fry on medium heat in a little oil until light brown. Drain on paper towels. Store in refrigerator.

Serve cold, sliced in half with thin sliced brown bread and butter and a little chutney.

Sausage Rolls

Flaky Pastry:
1 pound flour
¼ teaspoon salt
1½ cups margarine or shortening
water to bind

Filling:
1½ pounds of sausage meat
1 egg with little milk to brush on pastry
Oven 450°F

Pastry:
Sieve flour and salt; rub in ½ of the shortening, bind with water to an elastic consistency. Roll out to an oblong shape. Divide the remaining fat into tiny pieces. Cover 2/3 of the pastry with 1/4-teaspoon knobs of fat and fold pastry like an envelope. Roll out and repeat the folding using the remaining shortening.

Filling:
Roll the sausage meat into long strips, about half an inch thick. Roll pastry 1/4" thick and cut into strips wide enough to enclose a strip of sausage, seal the edge with beaten eggs and water. Cut into 1 ½" lengths and brush with egg mixture. Put three slits in the top of each sausage roll and bake on a non-greased cookie sheet for 12 minutes.

Lower oven to 350°F and cook for another 5 minutes or until pastry is golden.

Sausage rolls can be served hot or cold and make a delicious cocktail savory.

Sausage rolls are traditionally served on Christmas morning with a glass of sherry and often with miniature mince pies.

DINNER

Dinners in England are basically similar to dinners in America, the different courses depending on the time available and meal desired.

Dinners at home always used to be 'meat and two veggies', but things have moved on since then. Ethnic dishes such as Indian are now very popular, along with Chinese. Burger joints are as popular as they are here and fish and chip shops are still everywhere.

Dinner in a 'posh' inn or hotel usually consists of a multitude of courses consisting of soup, fish, sorbet, meat, sweet, cheese and biscuits (crackers), coffee, each course being accompanied by the appropriate wine and finished with a liqueur. Dinner in a pub however is usually only one course, followed by a simple dessert or cheese and crackers.

Americans have a habit of serving delicious meals on cold plates. Hot dinner should <u>always</u> be served on warmed plates to avoid cooling the food. This is especially true when serving meats such as lamb, the fat from which tends to congeal when cold.

Salads should be served on cold side plates.

Hotel Maes-y-Neuadd, Harlech, Gwynedd, North Wales

The earliest references to the original house date back to the mid-fourteenth century. The house is referred to as Maes-y-Neuadd, "The Hall in the Field."

Osbourne Wyddel was an Irishman. His forefathers were Anglo-Normans. He was reputed to have settled at Maes-y-Neuadd and married Agatha, daughter of the King of Castile and niece to the Queen of Edward I. One of his family became Constable of Harlech Castle during the Wars of the Roses. In 1468, the gallantry of the defenders of the castle over a long siege gave rise to the Welsh anthem – "Men of Harlech".

The 18th century was a good period; the estate was rich with hundreds of tenant farmers paying rent and the house was extended to include a drawing room, which is now the restaurant.

(continued)

(Hotel Maes-y-Neuadd, continued)

Eventually economic changes meant that farms had to be sold to meet debts, and the land eventually disappeared.

The house had to be leased out a number of times to help raise money for essential repairs. William Kirkby, born in 1884, was destined to be the last "Squire of Maes-y-Neuadd".

In 1950 it became impracticable to keep Maes-y-Neuadd in the family and it was leased out to be converted into an hotel and then after two years sold to become what it is today.

Phone: 011 44 1766 780200   Fax: 011 44 1766 780211

Poached Sole with a Prawn Mousse

This recipe is one of Peter Jackson's, the Chef Patron of the Hotel Maes-y-Neuadd, Harlech, North Wales, who is also manager of the Welsh National Culinary Team. Peter has cooked for the Queen, Prince Charles (Prince of Wales) and various Heads of State at the openings of the Welsh Assembly and other functions.

Mousse	Sauce
5 Fillets of Sole	*½ ounce butter*
3 ounce peeled jumbo shrimp	*1 chopped shallot*
1 dash of Cognac	*1 fl. ounce dry Vermouth*
1 egg white	*2 fl. ounce double cream*
Juice of ½ Lemon	*4 ounce Fish stock*
3 fl. ounce Double Cream	
Serves Four	

Mousse:
Blend <u>one</u> fillet of sole, the prawns, cognac, lemon juice and egg white until smooth. Add the cream and blend again. When very smooth, season and chill.

Sauce:
Melt the butter, add the shallots and cook until soft. Add the Vermouth and reduce in volume by ¾: add the stock and reduce again. Add cream and reduce by ½. Season to taste. Keep warm.

Gently flatten out the remaining sole fillets and place each one on an individual piece of cling film (Seran wrap). Spread the prawn mousse over and roll up tightly with the film. Poach in salted water for 15 minutes.

Divide the sauce between four plates. Unwrap the sole and cut into four. Place on the sauce.

Garnish with asparagus or herbs.

Lamb Curry With Rice

1 pound lean lamb, cut into one-inch cubes
1 large onion, chopped finely
1 clove garlic
¼ cup oil
½ teaspoon salt
½ teaspoon pepper
1 tablespoon curry powder
1 tablespoon flour and a little water
1 apple cut into small pieces
1 cup water
Rice for 4 servings
Oven 350°F

Sauté the onion and garlic lightly in the oil. Set aside.

Brown the lamb and put in a casserole dish with the onion and garlic. Make a smooth paste with the flour, a little water and the curry powder then add the cup water and stir well, then pour over the lamb in casserole. Add the apple.

Bake for 45 minutes covered. While curry dish is baking, prepare white or brown rice according to the directions on the package.

Serve lamb curry on a bed of rice along with mango or other sweet chutney, bread rolls and butter.

Welsh Winter Lamb

Milebrook House, Knighton, Powys, Wales

Serves 10 but is easily halved in quantity to serve 4 or 5
4½ lbs lean trimmed lamb
5 cups sliced onion
1 stick butter, clarified
3 or 4 fat cloves of garlic
1 lb bacon
¼ cup olive oil
1 small head of celery, thinly sliced
1 leek, sliced
10 ounce carrot, coarsely grated
Juice and zest of 1 orange
¼ cup parsley (plus another ¼ cup for later)
1 teaspoon rosemary, pounded with 1 teaspoon each of juniper
berries and rock salt
½ pint red wine
2 tablespoons flour
2 cups lamb stock
21 ounce tomatoes, liquidized
7 ounce dried kidney beans, soaked overnight, rinsed and strained
4-5 bay leaves
Oven 375°F

You need a lot of ingredients, but the result pays off. Make ahead and add a little water when reheating to avoid scorching. The water evaporates so you'll still have the right consistency.

Marinate the lamb overnight with the celery, herbs and spices, juice, zest and wine. Strain and save the liquid.

Roast the lamb pieces in a hot oven, seal, reserve. Cut the sliced bacon into postage stamp sized pieces and fry lightly in the oil so the pieces separate and don't stick together; cook the kidney beans in the lamb stock and reserve both.

Sweat the onions, leeks and garlic in the butter, and then add the flour and all the liquids. Adjust the seasoning, then add the lamb and vegetables and cook in a moderate oven until tender. Add the cooked kidney beans, cool rapidly and refrigerate.

Roast Beef and Yorkshire Pudding

The first Yorkshire pudding dates back to the middle ages. It was called "Dripping Pudding" and served as a first course. The batter mixture was placed under a spit were the meat would be roasting and the drippings would fall into the batter. Because times were hard and folks were poor, the men who worked endless hours in the woolen mills (the prime industry in Yorkshire) ate the meat and the rest of the family had to be content with the pudding and drippings from the roast.

I have always served Yorkshire pudding as a first course with gravy made from the meat juices. I rarely cook the pudding in a large pan as my mother did, because it's so easy to cook in muffin pans. Americans serve this recipe as Popovers.

Serves 6.

Roast Beef	**Yorkshire pudding**
4 pounds rib roast	*¾ cup flour*
2 tablespoons oil	*½ teaspoon salt*
	¾ cup milk
	1 tablespoon water
	2 eggs

Oven 450°F

Place the beef, fat side up, in a roasting pan and coat it with the oil. If you like your beef rare, it should cook for 1¼ hours and a meat thermometer should register between 130°F and 140°F. If you prefer it medium to well done, it should cook for 1½ hours and a meat thermometer should register between 150°F and 160°F. Baste the meat frequently while it is cooking.

While the meat is cooking, prepare the batter for the Yorkshire. Sift the flour and salt into a mixing bowl. Make a well in the center and add the milk and the water gradually, beating continuously with a wooden spoon.

In a separate bowl, beat the eggs until fluffy. Add them to the flour mixture. Beat until bubbles rise to the surface. Refrigerate for ½ hour or longer. Beat the batter frequently until you are ready to put it in the oven.

(continued)

(Roast Beef and Yorkshire Pudding, continued).

When the meat is cooked, remove it from the pan and place it on a warm platter. Cover with aluminum foil and let stand for 25 minutes before carving to let the juices retract into the meat. Drain a little fat from the meat drippings and spoon an equal amount into each muffin cup.

Put the muffin pan in a very hot oven to heat the fat until it is smoking hot.

Re-beat the batter once again and pour it quickly into the really hot fat in the pan. Bake it in the oven for 10 minutes at 450°F, then reduce the heat to 350°F and cook it for an additional 15 minutes, until batter is well risen and has turned a golden brown. (<u>Do not open the oven door while the pudding is cooking</u>.) Serve immediately from the pan in which it has been cooked.

Serve the meal with Horseradish Sauce, lots of vegetables and oven-roasted potatoes.

Note: In England, Sunday dinner, eaten at around mid-day usually involves a roast of some kind and is considered the best meal of the week.

English Shepherd's Pie

4 large potatoes, boiled and mashed, with
1 clove fresh garlic finely chopped
2 tablespoons margarine or butter, and
1 teaspoon Tabasco sauce
1 pound lean ground beef
4 large carrots, sliced into ½" rounds
2 tablespoons cooking oil
1 large onion chopped finely
1 tablespoon Worcestershire sauce
½ teaspoon salt
½ teaspoon pepper
2 beef bouillon cubes dissolved in 2 cups of boiling water.
1 tablespoon flour
½ pound grated cheddar cheese
Oven 350°F

Sauté the onions and garlic in oil in skillet until transparent. Push to the side of the skillet. Brown the beef. Add the carrots, Worcestershire sauce, salt and pepper and stir all the ingredients together. Cook for 10 minutes.

Mix flour and a little water to make a paste then add the bouillon liquid to flour and stir well. Add it to the skillet. Cook on medium heat for a few minutes more, until the mixture is thick and bubbly.

Put the meat mixture in a deep 8" casserole dish. Bake for 60 minutes on middle shelf, covered. If liquid is low, stir in a little more hot water.

Cook potatoes, drain and add a dash of Tabasco before mashing. Spread potatoes over the top. Sprinkle with grated cheese. Bake a further 15 minutes until cheese is melted and slightly browned.

Garnish with sliced tomatoes and serve hot.

Dalhousie Castle, Edinburgh, Scotland

Dalhousie Castle is steeped in history. All around guests will find fascinating reminders of its rich and often turbulent past.

The Ramsays of Dalhousie built the castle, which is full of interesting historical items, over 700 years ago. The Ramsays were a noble Scottish family descended from Simundus de Ramseia, who in about 1140 followed Kind David I to Scotland from the Huntingdonshire village of Ramsay.

The Castle has remained in the possession of one family longer than any other castle in Scotland. It stands peacefully amongst the rolling Midlothian countryside.

The fascinating story of the Ramsays, their long links with Scottish History and contributions abroad play an integral part in the enchantment of the Castle.

Phone: 011 44 1878 820153   Fax: 011 44 1875 821936

Scottish Shepherds Pie

Sheep are plentiful in the Highlands of Scotland where hill farming is still quite common. A lot of the Highlanders' meat dishes consequently use lamb instead of beef. Because lamb is not as popular in America as beef, I have included a recipe for English Shepherds Pie (page 83), which is made with ground beef.

> *1 lb ground lamb*
> *1½ lb potatoes*
> *2 small carrots, diced*
> *1 oz flour*
> *1 tablespoon tomato purée*
> *1 oz butter*
> *4 tablespoons milk*
> *1 large onion*
> *1 oz mushrooms*
> *Bay leaf*
> *1 cup lamb or beef stock*
> *½ cup grated cheese for the topping*
> *Oven 400°F*

Boil the potatoes for 20 minutes until tender. Mash (cream) the potatoes with the butter and milk.

Sauté the lamb with the chopped onion, bay leaf, mushroom and carrots for ten minutes.

Stir the flour into the mixture and add the stock and tomato purée. When the mixture starts to thicken, cover and simmer gently for about 25 minutes.

Remove the bay leaf. Place the mixture in a baking dish and cover with the mashed potatoes. Sprinkle the grated cheese on top and cook for 15 to 25 minutes.

Serve with lots of fresh vegetables.

Lancashire Hot Pot

This dish was popular in my family for Monday lunch, as the meat needs no browning and it is quick and easy to prepare. Monday was wash-day, we had no washing machine so it was an all-day procedure with little time left to prepare lunch.

3 large potatoes, sliced into 1/4" rounds
1 large onion sliced into rounds
2 pounds stewing steak, cut into 1" cubes
½ cup flour, mixed with pinch salt and pepper
¼ cup oil
½ crushed garlic clove
2 beef bouillon cubes dissolved in 2 cups hot water
1 teaspoon salt
1 teaspoon pepper
½ teaspoon thyme
Oven 350°F

Roll the cubed meat into the flour and place a layer in a deep 8- or 9-inch casserole dish. Add a layer of sliced onion. Add garlic. Sprinkle with a little of the salt, pepper and thyme.

Add a layer of sliced potatoes. Repeat with meat, then onion, finishing with potatoes. Add the remaining salt, pepper and thyme.

Pour the dissolved beef cube liquid over the top and the oil last. Cook for 1½ hours, middle shelf.

Place on a cookie sheet or silver foil, to catch any liquid that may spill over.

This dish is traditionally served with Brussels sprouts and baked carrots topped with fresh parsley.

Moat House Hotel, Stafford, Staffordshire

Located in a spectacular canal side setting in the village of Acton Trussell, just outside Stafford, the Moat House Hotel is a delightful 15th century moated manor house.

The beautiful moat house hotel is a grade II listed moated manor house built in the 15th century and steeped in history. In fact, the mound on which the house was built is a 'scheduled ancient monument' - a reflection of its historic importance.

The Moat House is probably best known for its fine dining with the conservatory restaurant winning the coveted best restaurant in Staffordshire (AA) as well as 2 AA rosettes plus hotel of the year 2000 (Heart Of England Tourist Board). When motoring was in its infancy, the AA (Automobile Association) would grade inns and restaurants in their handbook so that their members would know the best places to stop for a meal.

Phone: 011 44 1785 712217   Fax: 011 44 1785 715344

Confit of Pork Fillet with Creamed Cabbage, Apple Puree and Thyme Jus.

from the Moat House, Senior Sous Chef, Ian Coleman

16-ounce pork belly
½ pound shredded green cabbage
1½ pound pork fillet trimmed
Apple purée (see recipe below)
2 tablespoons sugar
1¼ cup chicken stock
1 pint dry white wine
10 sage leaves
4 shallots, minced
3 strands of thyme
2/3 cup double cream
½ pound unsalted butter

Confit mixture
2 pints goose fat
5 garlic cloves
2 bay leaves
Veal stock
8 slices bacon
Oven 450°F

First make the confit. Melt the fat in the oven; add the stock, herbs and spices. Place the tied pork belly into the fat (ask your butcher to tie it for you). Cover with tin foil. Turn the oven down to 300°F. Cook for at least four hours or until tender.

Apple purée: Cut four apples (Granny Smith) in half and core. Sprinkle with a little sugar. Place on a baking tray and bake until soft at 375°F. Scoop out flesh, pass through a sieve and season slightly (may need more sugar)

(continued)

(Pork confit continued)

Pork fillet: Cut each pork fillet into four and wrap each piece of meat with two slices of bacon. Season lightly. Wrap in cling film and put in fridge for at least two hours.
Blanch the cabbage, then cook in a little butter, drain, add cream, reduce and season.

Make the jus: Sweat the minced shallots in a little butter with a strand of thyme. Deglaze with white wine and reduce until four fifths. Add veal stock and reduce by at least one third, then pass through a fine sieve. Put back onto the heat, add a knob of butter and check seasoning.

Take the pork belly and slice into four equal slices. Pan fry in a little olive oil and add some chicken stock. Place in oven at 375°F and cook until glazed.

Seal the pork fillet in a pan, season, and cook in oven for 12 to 15 minutes or until cooked.

Warm through the apple purée.

Place the warm cabbage mixture in the middle of four warmed plates. Place the glazed pork belly on top, then the purée, and then the pork fillet.

Rabbit Pie

1 bay leaf
8 bacon slices
1 pound mushrooms, sliced lengthwise
3 leeks, cleaned and chopped into 1 inch pieces.
1 rabbit (about 2 lbs) cut into small portions
Salt and pepper,
3 tablespoons chopped parsley
3 medium sized potatoes, peeled sliced into ¼ inch rounds.
1 tablespoon vinegar
Chicken broth
¼ cup flour
Oven 325°F.

Soak rabbit in equal parts of water and vinegar overnight.

Make pastry from recipe from *page 43* and refrigerate.

Place the bay leaf on the bottom of a large ovenproof dish with 4 pieces of bacon on the top plus half the mushrooms and half the leeks. Add salt and pepper and a little of the parsley.

Put the rabbit pieces on top and cover with remaining mushrooms and leeks.

Make a broth with water and chicken stock and thicken with a little flour. Pour over the rabbit pieces then add the potatoes so the other vegetables are completely covered. Season again with salt and pepper and chopped parsley.

Put the remaining bacon on top and sprinkle the vinegar over the dish.

Cook for 1½ hours covered with foil or a lid. Take out of the oven and set aside to cool a little while preparing the pastry.

Roll out the pastry to fit the top of the dish, make a hole in the center.

Cook at 375°F for 20 –25 minutes until pastry is golden brown.

Bubble and Squeak

If you have vegetables and cooked plain potatoes (without milk, cream or butter added) left over, this is a wonderful way to make another dish which is really tasty and is traditionally served with cold leftover turkey, chicken or the Sunday roast pork, beef or lamb.

4 cups cooked mashed potatoes, plain
4 cups cooked cabbage
or Brussels sprouts chopped up small.
Salt
Fresh pepper
4 tablespoons olive oil

Mix the potatoes and vegetables. Heat the oil in a large frying pan and add the cooked vegetables and potatoes.

Press and turn frequently to brown all over.

Serve on hot plates with cold cuts of meat and chutney.

Note: The name is derived from the bubbling and squeaking the potatoes and vegetables make when they are cooking in the pan.

The Bull Hotel, Long Melford, Suffolk

The Bull Hotel

The broad main street of Long Melford is the longest high street in East Anglia, and the historic Bull is its centerpiece and has been for 500 years. It is believed that a wealthy wool merchant built the Bull, because in the fifteenth century the town was an important wool town and the center of a big cloth making industry. The Woolmen were the richest in the country and would certainly have been in a position to build a fine mansion such as the Bull. The shape of the house bears out this theory for the main block could have been a residence while the two wings and other buildings at the back would have been suitable for warehouses and workshops.

By 1580 it had become an inn; the sign of the Bull was displayed outside its walls and its doors were open to travelers. For more than a century the fine timbered frontage which it now displays was hidden from view by a flat brick front, erected probably with the idea of giving the old place an up-to-date appearance in keeping with the newly built Georgian inns of the coaching era. It was thought for many years that the original frontage had been pulled down, but in 1935 it was discovered hidden from view behind nine inch thick brickwork which, when removed, revealed a magnificent example of fifteenth century architecture.

Phone: 011 44 1787 378494   Fax: 011 44 1787 880307

Breast Of Guinea Fowl in a Red Wine and Mushroom Sauce.

from the Bull Hotel, Long Melford, Suffolk

A Traditional Suffolk Recipe

> *Serves 2*
> *2 guinea fowl breasts about 6 oz each*
> *Seasoned flour*
> *2 cups button mushrooms*
> *1 cup finely diced onions*
> *¼ stick butter*
> *2 tablespoons olive oil*
> *¼ cup port wine*
> *¼ cup red wine*
> *½ cup chicken gravy*
> *Oven 350°F*

Melt the butter with the vegetable oil in a frying pan. Dust the guinea fowl breast with flour. Add to the pan with the diced onions and mushrooms.

Cook until the onions are clear. When the fowl is 2/3 cooked, add the port, red wine, gravy and chicken seasoning.

Serve with new boiled potatoes and fresh vegetables.

Note: Cornish Game Hens work well for this recipe.

Paella

¼ *teaspoon saffron powder*
4 *tablespoons olive oil*
2 *medium size onions, chopped finely*
2 *cloves garlic, crushed and chopped*
2½ *cups of chicken stock*
2 *cups of prawns or shrimp, peeled*
3 *chicken breasts, skinned and diced*
2 *skinned tomatoes chopped*
1 *cup peas*
1 *cup long grain rice*
½ *teaspoon salt*
½ *teaspoon pepper*
¼ *cup fresh chopped parsley*

In a skillet, sauté the onions and garlic in oil until transparent, and then add the diced chicken and rice and stir.

In a bowl, stir the saffron powder into the chicken stock, and then pour into the skillet.

Cook on low heat stirring often for 20 minutes or so, (until rice is tender and all liquid is absorbed). Add the shrimp or prawns, peas, tomatoes and seasonings. Toss gently and cook for five minutes more until shrimps are just cooked.

Although this dish is Spanish, it is often found on pub menus.

Note: mussels can be used instead of shrimp.

The Old Bell Hotel, Malmesbury, Wiltshire

The Old Bell stands on the top of a hill and, apart from the Abbey, is the highest building in Malmesbury. It is not surprising, therefore, that there were fortifications on the site many hundreds of years ago. There was probably a Saxon castle, but as these were generally built of wood any evidence of occupation prior to the 12th century has now disappeared.

Bishop Roger Poore of Sarum, probably erected the stone fortification about 1130, in the reign of Henry I. The only certain remains of this castle are in the wall immediately to the west of the gazebo at the end of the garden. One local historian believes that the central part of The Old Bell was formed from the castle after the grant of King John in 1216 to demolish it.

However, the claim to be England's oldest hotel rests on the premise that an almost completely new building was erected around 1220 by Walter Loring (the Abbott from 1208 to 1244). Its function was to entertain important guests; the Abbey was then one of the most important seats of learning in England.

Phone: 011 44 1666 822344   Fax: 011 44 1666 825145

Sole Véronique

from The Old Bell Hotel, Malmesbury, Wiltshire

Serves 4
3 medium sole fillets
salt and pepper to taste
1 cup dry white wine
3 tablespoons butter
¼ cup flour
¼ pint milk
1 cup white seeded grapes
Oven 375°F

Roll each fillet, tail end first and secure with a toothpick.

Butter a baking pan and arrange the fillets in the pan. Sprinkle with salt and pepper and pour the wine over the fish.

Cook uncovered for about 10 minutes in the oven. Lift the fish carefully on to a warm serving dish.

Meanwhile, heat the butter, stir in the flour and a measured half pint of liquid made up of juices from the fish and milk. Bring to the boil and cook, stirring until smooth and thick. Taste and adjust the seasoning as required.

Pour over the fish and decorate with the grapes.

Stuffed Veal with Sherry Sauce

Serves 4
1 pound of sliced veal, pounded thin.

Stuffing:
1 small onion, grated
¼ cup margarine
½ cup soft breadcrumbs
1 tablespoon chopped parsley
pinch salt, pepper and thyme
1 egg
4 slices of bacon chopped
½ pound fresh mushrooms, sliced

Sauce:
1 cup plain yogurt
1 tablespoon chopped parsley
2 teaspoons capers
2 tablespoons cooking sherry
1 teaspoon hot mustard
pinch salt and pepper
Oven 425°F

Mix the bacon, mushrooms, parsley, onion, margarine, breadcrumbs, egg and seasonings in a bowl. Stir until mixture binds.

Brush 4 squares of silver foil with oil. Lay a slice of veal on each one and put a ½ cup of bacon mixture on top. Close the foil around each slice to make a pocket.

Bake in a shallow casserole dish for 30 minutes.

Sauce:
Put the yogurt into a double boiler with parsley, salt, pepper and sherry. Heat slowly then add capers and mustard.

Unwrap the pockets carefully and serve on individual plates with the sauce and a lemon wedge, small salad and bread.

The Oak Inn, Lyndhurst, Hampshire

Built in the late 18th century as a cider house, the Oak Inn was one of a number of hostelries that serviced the coach traveling public en-route from Ringwood to Southampton and beyond. Additionally, the Oak would have supplied the local farm laborers who worked on the many farms in the area.

A visit to this inn will transport you to a welcoming, relaxed atmosphere where you can enjoy some of the finest food and ales that the New Forest has to offer.

Lying just off the A35, The Oak Inn sits in the idyllic quiet village of Bank, a mile or so from Lyndhurst, the capital of the New Forest. Because the pub faces the open forest, ponies can be seen grazing at most times of the year, much to the delight of visitors. Twilight diners may catch glimpses of the herds of red and fallow deer as they settle down for the evening.

Phone: 011-44-23-0028-2350

Steak and Kidney Pudding

from the Oak Inn, Lyndhurst, Hampshire

1 pound stewing steak, cubed
2 small lamb's (or beef) kidneys, chopped
2 teaspoons flour
½ cup beef stock or bouillon cube and water
¼ teaspoon pepper
¼ teaspoon salt

Pastry:
2 cups flour
¼ pound shortening
4 tablespoons water
2 teaspoons baking powder
Oven 400°F

Discard any gristle or skin from the kidneys. Mix the chopped kidneys and steak together with seasoned flour. Set aside.

Make pastry by mixing flour, shortening, salt and baking powder with the water to make a soft dough. Roll thinly and use three quarters of it to line a 2-pint deep bowl (not metal).

Put the meat mixture and stock to half way up the side of the dish. Use the remaining pastry to form a lid and press the edges firmly together with a little water. Cover with wax paper and foil. Steam in a pan of water for 4-5 hours.

Serve hot with green vegetables.

This dish can also be served as a pie. Put the steak and kidney mixture in a deep-dish casserole with regular flaky pastry - on the top only and bake for 1½ hours.

The Pandora Inn, Restronguet Creek, Falmouth, Cornwall

Some say that the Inn is named after the H.M.S. Pandora, the ship sent to find the mutineers of H.M.S. Bounty of Captain Bligh fame. Others say that it was named after a sailing schooner of the same name that worked out of Restronguet. Whatever the truth, this historic Inn is well worth a visit. There are good facilities for mooring alongside, but keep an eye on the tide.

Parts of the building date back to the 13th Century when there was a farm on the site; the Restronguet Estate Accounts for the year 1468 state that the rent was 8s 4d (75c) a year.

The restaurant is housed above the award-winning pub on the second floor of a thatched 13th century building. The menu caters for all tastes, including vegetarian, but concentrates on fresh, locally caught seafood.

Phone: 011 44 1326 372678.   Fax: 011 44 1326 372678.

Restronguet Fish Pie

From The Pandora Inn, Restronguet, Falmouth, Cornwall

Serves 2
½ pound white fish – cod is best
2 ounce peeled prawns
1 hard boiled egg, chopped
½ cup chopped onion
2 ounces butter
2 tablespoons flour
2 cups milk
¼ cup chopped parsley
1 cup mashed potatoes
½ cup grated cheddar cheese

Boil fish and remove bones. Add prawns, parsley and chopped hard-boiled egg.

Mix in the béchamel sauce, spoon into an ovenproof dish, top with mashed potatoes and add the grated cheese on top.

For the Béchamel sauce:
Melt butter in a medium size saucepan and sauté the chopped onion until transparent.

Stir in the flour and make a roux, gradually add the milk and the wine. Bring to the boil stirring continuously. Season to taste.

Sole fillets with Vanilla Nage (Sauce) and Seared Scallops

from the Moat House Hotel, Stafford

3 whole lemon sole, filleted, skinned and halved
12 fresh scallops
2 cups vanilla nage (make in advance)
1 carrot cut into fine strips
½ English cucumber, cut into 12 pieces
Chervil
12 small, boiled, new potatoes
¼ lb unsalted butter
1 teaspoon olive oil
1 lb washed spinach

Vanilla Nage

1 small onion, chopped	*1 leek, chopped*
1 celery stick, finely chopped	*3 carrots, chopped*
4 cloves garlic, skinned	*3 lemon slices*
8 white peppercorns	*½ vanilla pod, split*
1 star anise	*2½ pints cold water*
1 cup white wine	
Sprig parsley, tarragon, and chervil.	

First make the vanilla nage (sauce.) Place all the chopped vegetables in a pan with the water and bring to the boil. Add all herbs, spices and vanilla and simmer for two minutes. Take from the heat, add the wine and set aside in the pan for at least four hours.

Sear the sole fillets in a little oil in a hot pan and season. Remove. Sear the scallops for 30 seconds each side and season. Remove.

Thicken the nage with a little unsalted butter to emulsify. Dry the spinach, season and arrange on four plates. Warm the potatoes and cucumber. Divide the sole, potatoes, cucumber and scallops between each plate, dress with the nage and carrot strips.

Faggots

Faggots is a very old fashioned dish that used to be a popular way to use up the odd bits and pieces left over from a pig. Some butchers still prepare their own faggots, but this is becoming increasingly rare. To be authentic, Faggots, also known as Poor Man's Goose or Savory Duck, should be cooked in the caul (the fatty veil that covers the pig's abdominal organs) and made in the shape of sausages.

However, this recipe does without the caul and is a lot simpler to prepare.

> *4 ounces liver*
> *8 slices bacon*
> *6 medium-sized onions*
> *1¼ cups water*
> *3 cups breadcrumbs soaked in 1 cup water*
> *½ teaspoon sage*
> *Salt*
> *Freshly ground black pepper*
> *Oven 250°F.*

Chop the liver, bacon and onions into small pieces. Cook the bacon and onions together in a pan over low heat for 5 minutes. Add the liver and water. Simmer the mixture for 15 minutes. Add the soaked breadcrumbs and the sage. Season with a little salt and pepper and mix thoroughly. Turn into a well-greased, square, baking pan. Cut into squares and bake for 45 minutes. Serve cold.

Cheese and Onion Hotpot

1 pound potatoes, peeled and thinly sliced
1 pound onions, sliced thinly
2 cups cheddar cheese, grated
pinch of salt and pepper
¼ cup melted margarine
½ cup milk
Oven 350°F

Put layers of potatoes, cheese and onions into a medium size casserole dish. Season each layer and brush with melted margarine.

Repeat layers ending in potatoes. Pour the milk over the mixture and bake for 1¼ hours.

This is great for a late supper dish because it is meatless and easy to digest.

About Onions:
Onions may be eaten raw, broiled, boiled, baked, creamed, steamed fried, French-fried and pickled. They are a versatile vegetable used in many recipes.

Popular varieties include Yellow & White Sweet Spanish, Yellow and White Bermuda, Southport Red Globe, Texas Grano, Vidalia Sweet, Red Hamburger, Supersweet and the most popular of all, Walla Walla Sweet.

Toad In The Hole

Serves 4
1 cup flour
½ teaspoon salt
2 cups milk
1 egg
8 beef or pork sausages
¼ cup light oil
1 package of gravy mix or your own gravy
4 servings of peas
Oven 450°F

Batter Mixture:
Mix flour and salt together in mixing bowl. Drop egg in the center, add milk and mix well. Leave for 2 hours, beating well every so often. Mixture will thicken as it sits, so add a little water to thin it down and let stand for a further 30 minutes.

Pour the oil into an 8 inch baking pan or casserole dish, and heat in oven until sizzling hot. Pour batter mixture into the hot oil, distribute the sausages around the pan and return to oven immediately. Put a cookie sheet on shelf below to catch spillage. Do not open oven door for 30 minutes then check to make sure batter has risen and is golden brown.

Batter should come out of the pan easily. Serve on warm plates with peas and a little beef gravy poured over the top.

This is the batter used for Yorkshire Pudding (page 81) without the sausage of course.

Exeter Stew and Dumplings

Stew:
4 tablespoons oil
2 pounds of sirloin steak cut into cubes
2 onions sliced
½ cup flour
1 teaspoon gravy browning
4 cups water or beef stock
½ teaspoon salt
½ teaspoon pepper
1 teaspoon marjoram
4 carrots diced

In stew pot or deep skillet, sauté the onion in oil until light brown. Push to side. Add meat and brown on high heat. Make a paste with the flour, gravy browning, water, salt and pepper. Pour into the pan; add carrot and marjoram.

Bring to the boil and simmer for 3/4 hour. Make dumplings.

Dumplings:
1 cup flour
2 tablespoons lard or shortening (or suet)
1 tablespoon parsley, chopped
¼ teaspoon salt
¼ teaspoon pepper
½ teaspoon baking powder

Mix all the ingredients together with a little water to make a paste. Shape into eight dumplings and drop into the skillet with stew. Simmer for another hour.

Serve in soup bowls with a small dinner salad on the side.

The Swan Inn, Lavenham, Suffolk

Lavenham is the finest example of a medieval wool town in England. In Tudor times, Lavenham was said to be the fourteenth wealthiest town in England, despite its small size. Its fine timber-framed buildings and beautiful church, built on the success of the wool trade, make it a fascinating place to visit.

Although Lavenham goes back to Saxon times, it is best known as a medieval wool town. It was granted its market charter in 1257 and started exporting its famous blue broadcloth as far afield as Russia.

As well as its many historic buildings, Lavenham is also blessed with good pubs, fine places to eat and fascinating antique shops.

The Swan Inn is a fine example of late-medieval, half-timbered architecture and is just one of three hundred listed buildings in Lavenham. Its award-winning restaurant, which specializes in using fresh local produce, makes this a popular local eating-place.

Phone: 011 44 870 4008116

Lamb and Mushroom Pie

from the Swan Inn, Lavenham, Suffolk

Pubs usually serve this type of pie in individual dishes but this dish can be made in a regular 9" pie plate.

1 red onion
4 oz mushrooms
¼ stick butter
1 lb lamb
½ pint beef stock
2 tablespoons Worcestershire sauce
salt and pepper
pinch mace
4 oz puff pastry or short crust (page 124)
1 egg, beaten
Oven 400°F

Peel and chop the onion. Wash and roughly chop the mushrooms. Fry both gently in the butter until soft.

Cut the meat in one-inch pieces and add to the pan. Cook for 10 minutes. Add the stock, seasoning and Worcestershire sauce. Cover and simmer for 20 minutes.

Meanwhile make the pastry and set aside.

Place the cooked meat mixture in individual pie dishes such as 4 inch high, 7 oz. ramekins.

Roll pastry fairly thin and cover the dishes. Trim the edges and flute, make a hole in the pastry in the middle. Brush with the beaten egg and bake in the center of the oven for 15 minutes. Reduce the oven to 350°F and bake for a further 15 minutes.

Serve with braised celery and carrots.

Roast Pheasant

Serves 4 - 6
3 ounces butter
3 tablespoons flour
1 brace (pair) of Pheasant
1 teaspoon sage
4 bacon slices
1 bunch watercress
1 small onion, finely chopped
1 cup mushrooms, finely sliced
1 cup sherry
1 cup meat stock
Salt
Freshly ground black pepper
Oven 400°F.

Melt 2 ounces of the butter in a roasting pan. Sprinkle 2 tablespoons of flour over the pheasants and gently brown them over medium heat for 2 or 3 minutes. Put half of the remaining butter and the sage inside each pheasant.

Put the pheasants breast-up in the roasting pan and cover with the bacon slices. Roast the birds for 35 minutes, basting from time to time. Be careful not to overcook them or they will become dry.

Transfer the cooked pheasants to a warm serving dish, surround them with watercress and let them rest for at least 10 minutes before carving. Spoon out most of the cooking fat from the roasting pan, leaving just enough in which to brown the onion. Cook the onions until they have turned soft and brown; add the mushrooms and toss for a few minutes. Add the remaining tablespoon of flour and gradually pour in the sherry and the stock, stirring continually.

Bring the mixture to a boil and simmer for 10 minutes. Remove any froth, season to taste with salt and pepper and serve in a gravy boat. Serve it with a generous amount of Bread Sauce (page 117).

Homemade Sage and Onion Stuffing (Dry Dressing)

Stuffing a bird with dressing enhances its flavor. You should aim for half a cup of stuffing for each pound of bird.

The breadcrumbs should come from day-old dry bread. Use a rolling pin and wax paper to make really fine crumbs and herbs really make stuffing tasty so don't be afraid to experiment.

> ½ cup chopped onion
> 1 cup chopped celery
> 1 stick of butter
> 3 tablespoons chopped parsley
> 3½ cups dry breadcrumbs (not cubes)
> Salt and pepper to taste
> 1 tablespoon sage or thyme, not both

Mix the breadcrumbs, salt, pepper and sage in a bowl.

Sauté the onions and celery in the butter until opaque and soft. Drain the butter and save.

Add the sautéed onions and celery to the breadcrumb and mix thoroughly.

Pour some of the butter into the bird cavity to line it, add the stuffing mix and pour the remaining butter over the mix.

Pease Pudding

Pease Pudding hot,
Pease Pudding cold,
Pease Pudding in the pot
Nine days old

> *8 oz dried split peas, soaked*
> *1 small, peeled and halved onion*
> *1 bunch fresh herbs, tied together*
> *½ pint water*
> *1 egg*
> *Salt*
> *Freshly ground black pepper*

Drain the peas and put them in a pan with the onion, herbs, pepper and water. Bring to the boil, cover the pan and simmer until the peas are tender - about an hour. Check during the cooking, stir occasionally, and add a little more boiling water if the peas are drying out before they are cooked. Remove the herbs.

Beat the peas into a smooth purée, or liquidize them in a blender and beat in the egg and seasoning. The purée should resemble a thick paste.

Turn the purée into a greased and floured mixing bowl. Cover it tightly with aluminum foil and tie it securely with string around the rim. Put in a saucepan with about 2 inches of water to steam, and boil for 1 hour.

Serve directly from the bowl.

The Old Hall Inn, Sea Palling, Norwich, Norfolk

The Old Hall Inn is a centuries old manor house full of charm and character, with wooden beams and an inglenook fireplace.

It even boasts its own ghost, 'The Grey Lady'!

The restaurant serves delicious homemade food and an à la carte menu which changes regularly. Lighter bites and lunchtime snacks are also available in the bar.

Phone: 011-44-1692-598-323   Fax: 011-44-1692-598-822

Fish and Chips

Serves 4
5 cups vegetable oil
1 cup peanut oil (stops the oil from smoking)
1 cup flour
¼ cup rice flour or yellow cornstarch
1 egg
1 ¼ cups amber ale
1 teaspoon salt
½ teaspoon white pepper
¼ teaspoon celery seed
2 pounds true cod fillets

Heat oil in a large pan.

Batter:
Mix the flour, rice flour and cornstarch in a separate bowl and set aside. Beat well together the egg, ale, celery seed, salt, pepper and then slowly whisk the egg mixture into the flour mixture until smooth. Batter should not be too thin.

Cut the fish into equal pieces and make sure that each piece is dry before dipping into the batter mix. Coat evenly.

Deep fry the fish in very hot oil for 5 – 7 minutes to make sure the fish is properly cooked, turn over to crisp on both sides.

Keep each piece separate in the cooking oil so they don't stick together.

Remove when golden brown and drain on paper towel.

Serve with crisply cooked French Fries, known as chips in England. (Traditionally, in England, potatoes for French fries are peeled, never cooked with the skin on.)

Pease Pudding is often served with fish and chips (page 111.)

Marinated Duck Breast

With Sweet Potato and Mushroom Hash
from Chef Peter Gorton, Horn of Plenty, Tavistock, Devon

Serves 4
4 duck breasts
Duck Marinade
Salt and freshly ground black pepper
10 oz firmly packed dark brown sugar
¼ cup rice wine vinegar
1 tablespoon Dijon mustard
1 teaspoon lemon juice
1½ teaspoons chopped fresh thyme
¼ cup peanut oil

To marinate the duck breasts:
Season the duck with salt and pepper and arrange in a single layer in a baking dish. Whisk together the sugar, vinegar, mustard, lemon juice, thyme and peanut oil. Pour over the duck and marinate in the refrigerator for at least 4 hours.

Sweet Potato Hash
Olive oil
¼ cup pine nuts
1lb assorted fresh mushrooms
2 shallots finely chopped
3 maris piper potatoes (baker potatoes), cut into ½ inch cubes
3 sweet potatoes cut into ½ inch cubes
½ large red onion finely chopped
2 cloves of garlic, finely chopped
(½ bunch of coriander optional)
(2 tablespoons balsamic vinegar optional)
Oven 375°F

(continued)

(Marinated Duck Breast, continued)

To Prepare the Hash
Spread the pine nuts on a baking sheet and toast for 5 minutes until golden brown, set aside.

Melt 1 tablespoon butter and 1 tablespoon of olive oil in a large pan, add half of the mushrooms and sauté over a high heat for 5 minutes or until golden and all the liquid has evaporated. Transfer to a bowl and repeat the process with the remaining butter and olive oil, add mushrooms, shallots and garlic to the pan and cook until they are translucent, season with salt and pepper. Set aside.

Bring 2 medium saucepans of salted water to a boil, cook the potatoes (bakers in one pan, sweet in the other) until just tender. Drain and transfer the potatoes into separate bowls.

Heat 1 tablespoon of peanut oil in a large pan, add the red onion and cook over a medium heat stirring for about 5 minutes. Add the baker potatoes and cook for about 5 minutes or until tender and golden brown and transfer them to a large bowl. Add the remaining oil to the pan and repeat the process with the sweet potatoes, finally add the mushroom mixture: adjust seasoning.

Remove duck from the marinade and drain well, reserving the marinade. Place the duck breasts in a large frying pan and sear until they are golden brown. Place on a baking tray and cook in 350°F oven for 6 minutes, allow to rest for 5 minutes then carve each breast into five pieces.

To Serve
Spoon some of the hash in the centre of each plate and top with a mound of fried sweet potato. Arrange the carved duck breast around the sweet potato hash and serve with a selection of green vegetables and a sauce of your choice.

Basic White Sauce

Makes 3 cups.
1½ ounces butter
4 tablespoons flour
3 cups milk
Salt
White pepper

Melt the butter in a heavy-bottomed pan over low heat. Add the flour and cook for about 2 minutes, stirring constantly with a wooden spoon. Gradually pour in the milk, continuing to stir until it is completely absorbed and you have a smooth white sauce. Season to taste with salt and pepper and simmer very gently for 10 to 15 minutes, stirring from time to time.

Parsley Sauce:

A delicate-flavored sauce that goes well with any kind of poached white fish. It is also frequently served with Smoked Haddock.

3 cups Basic White Sauce (as above)
1½ cup chicken stock
Juice of ½ lemon
4 tablespoons finely chopped parsley
Salt
White pepper

Prepare Basic White Sauce and add the chicken stock, lemon juice and parsley. Reheat the sauce and stir well. Season to taste with salt and pepper.

Anchovy Sauce

Serve this with any kind of poached white fish.

Makes 3 cups.
3 cups Basic White Sauce
2 ounces butter
3 tablespoons anchovy paste
1 cup heavy cream
Salt
Freshly ground black pepper

Prepare the Basic White Sauce (page 116.)

In a separate saucepan melt the butter over low heat. Add the anchovy paste and mix well. Gradually pour in the White Sauce and add the cream. Simmer over low heat for 10 minutes. Season to taste with salt and pepper and serve.

Bread Sauce

This delicately flavored sauce is usually served with roast chicken and other poultry.

1 small onion, peeled
3 whole cloves
salt & pepper
2 cups milk
2 tablespoons butter
1 cup fresh white bread crumbs
3 tablespoons cream (optional)

In a small saucepan boil the milk with the butter and stir in the breadcrumbs. Stud the onion with the cloves and place in the saucepan with the mixture. Simmer for fifteen minutes on low heat covered. Remove the onion and beat the sauce smooth. Season and leave on the stove (over a pan of hot water) to keep warm and stir in the cream immediately before serving.

The Nobody Inn, Doddiscombsleigh, Exeter, Devon

A Saxon, Alsi, held the town of Doddiscombsleigh which appeared as Terra Godeboldi in the Domesday Book of 1086,AD "being held by one Godbold the Bowman."

The Nobody Inn was originally known as *Popill Howse* and was one of a number of dwelling houses built in the 1500's on land owned by Ralph Doddescomb. His family had owned the land since 1216AD.

It is written that the Babb family purchased the land from Sir Ralph Doddescomb around 1522, then *Popill Howse* disappeared from the records for approximately a hundred years. It reappeared as being occupied by Stephen Diggines, 'The Carpenter', although it was owned by the Parr family. His son, also Stephen and the village carpenter, inherited occupancy of the house from his father and it was established as *The New Inn* by a William Diggines in the 1800's.

(continued)

(Nobody Inn history continued)

The inn was the village unofficial Church House and a meeting place for business and recreation where parish matters were settled.

The Diggines family continued to operate *The New Inn* through the 19th century. Thomas junior was the last Diggines to hold the Inn until his death in1910 when it passed to George Smaile.

According to local legend an unknown purchaser of the Inn was reputed to have closed and locked the doors and refused hospitality to weary travelers seeking bed or refreshment. They, upon receiving no answer to their knocking continued on their journeys in the belief that there was nobody in and "Nobody Inn" it has remained since.

Up to today it has continued as a privately owned Free House. (For Free House refer to page 9.)

This renowned 16th Century Inn is located in the west of England, six miles from Exeter and within a short drive from Dartmoor and the coast. It has long outlived its reputation for its inhospitable past and today's traveler is assured of a warm and genuine welcome.

The bar and cellar ranks with the finest in the country where traditionally brewed beer, local cider, one hundred and seventy whiskies, five hundred wines, fine ports and brandies and home-made mulled wine will satisfy the most obdurate palate.

Phone: 011 44 1647 252394   Fax: 011 44 1647 252978

Roast Duck with Orange Sauce

4 to 5 lbs oven ready duck
1 large onion, peeled and chopped small
2 oranges
1 tablespoon chopped parsley
1 level tablespoon gravy browning
2 tablespoons cornstarch
salt and pepper
Oven 375°F

Sprinkle the duck with salt and pepper and put the chopped onion inside the bird. Place the bird on a trivet in a roasting pan and roast for 20 minutes per pound plus 20 minutes over. Half way through the cooking, baste the duck and spoon out any surplus fat from the roasting pan.

Use the giblets to make the stock while the duck is roasting. Do this by putting the giblets in a pint of water and boiling for half an hour.

Grate the rind from one orange and squeeze the juice into a bowl along with the juice from the other orange.

When the duck is cooked, pour the surplus fat from the pan and set it aside.

Take the duck out of the pan and put on a warm serving dish. In the pan, add the gravy browning and cornstarch and stir into a paste. Place the pan over a gentle heat, add the grated orange rind, orange juice and stock and stir to make a smooth sauce.

Serve the duck on individual plates and pour a little of the sauce over each.

PUDDINGS

In Great Britain, the word pudding is used as a generic term for most after-dinner sweets. In some parts of the country you will also hear the terms "afters" to describe what the Americans know as desserts.

Most of the recipes here date back to my mother's childhood when suet was used a lot for puddings which sat like lead in one's stomach, especially the Queen of Puddings (page 128) and Spotted Dick (page 132).

Because suet is not readily available in America I have substituted it with shortening and given recipes for lighter desserts and sweets, which are easily made (and digested).

Although some of the recipes have changed in translation they remain basically the same, with the same wonderful names that often reflect the towns where they originated.

Just to confuse you further, not all puddings are desserts or sweets; for example, Steak and Kidney pudding (page 99) and Yorkshire Pudding (page 81) are both savory dishes.

Note: many English steamed puddings are served with hot custard, which is available in supermarkets as 'Birds Dessert Powder' or 'Edmonds Custard Powder'.

Bakewell Tart

From my friends "The Twins" who live in Derby.
Bakewell is a village near Derby in the English Midlands.

Pastry:
1 cup sifted flour
⅓ cup shortening
2 tablespoons water
½ teaspoon salt

Filling:
½ cup butter (1 stick)
½ cup sugar
1 tablespoon apricot jam
2 eggs
½ cup ground almonds
½ teaspoon vanilla extract
½ teaspoon almond extract

Glaze:
1 tablespoon powdered sugar
2 teaspoons lemon juice
Oven 375°F

Make pastry by mixing flour and salt. Blend half the shortening, cut finely with knife, until pastry looks like meal. Cut in the remaining shortening until mixture is course, like peas. Sprinkle with water a little at a time until pastry forms a dough. Roll and refrigerate while making the filling.

Filling:
Cream together the butter and sugar. Beat the eggs together before adding a little at a time to the butter/sugar mixture. Add almonds and vanilla and mix well.

Roll out pastry and line a 9-inch pie plate. Spread the jam over the pastry. Add filling. Mix sugar and lemon juice together in separate bowl and drizzle over the top as a glaze. Bake for 40 minutes in center of oven.

Apple Dumplings

10 apples
¾ cup sugar
1 tablespoon cinnamon
¼ cup butter
½ cup sliced almonds
Whipping cream for topping
Oven 425°F

Pastry:
Use the recipe for short crust pastry on page 124.

Filling:
Peel, core and cut up the apples. In a separate bowl, mix ½ cup of the sugar and cinnamon then stir into the cut apples.

Divide the pastry into two and roll out thin. Cut into 4-inch squares.

Put ¼ cup of the apple mixture into each pastry square and pinch the edges together to form a pouch. Brush with beaten egg. Sprinkle with remaining sugar and almonds.

Bake on cookie sheet for 10 minutes. Reduce heat to 350°F and bake for a further 25 minutes until pastry is golden.

Serve warm with cream.

About Apples:
There are many varieties of apples in this country but there are recommended uses for selected varieties. For pie: Golden Delicious and Newton Pippin are considered excellent. For baking whole, Rome Beauty is the best. For fresh salads, Red Delicious and for sauce, Gravenstein is highly recommended. There are many other delicious varieties to be recommended when eaten raw such as Gala, Jonagold and McIntosh, and for a really tart apple, the old standby Granny Smith is a winner.

Egg Custard

Short crust pastry (see below)
2 eggs
½ pint milk
2 tablespoons sugar
Nutmeg
9 inch Soufflé Dish
Oven 325°F

Line dish with pastry. Beat eggs, sugar together. Add milk and beat again. Pour into pastry case and sprinkle with nutmeg.

Bake 35 – 40 minutes until top is golden brown.

Short Crust Pastry

8oz plain flour (all purpose)
pinch of salt
2oz butter
2oz shortening
cold water to mix

Sift the flour and salt into a mixing bowl. Cut the butter and shortening into the flour and then rub between the fingertips until a fine breadcrumb consistency is achieved.

Gradually mix in cold water with a knife until the bowl comes clean and the pastry is not crumbly (too dry) or sticky (too wet).

Roll into a ball, put into a polythene bag and allow to "rest" in the refrigerator for 30 minutes before rolling out.

Crème Brûlée with Exotic Fruit Dice

from Chef Peter Gorton, The Horn of Plenty, Tavistock, Devon

Serves 4 – 6
1 ½ cups whipping cream
5 egg yolks
6 tablespoons sugar
1 vanilla bean, split lengthwise
Oven 325°F

Exotic Fruit Dice
1 kiwi, cut into small cubes
1 small mango, cut into small cubes
1 small papaya, cut into small cubes
1 small fresh pineapple, cut into small cubes
8 oz strawberries cut in half (optional)

Mix fruits together and set aside

Whisk yolks and sugar in medium bowl to blend. Scrape in seeds from vanilla bean. Gradually whisk the cream into the sugar. Divide mixture among 6 custard cups or 6 oz ramekins. Arrange custard cups in 13x9x2 inch baking pan. Pour enough hot water into pan to come halfway up sides of cups. Cover with foil to give steam.

Bake custards approximately 35-40 minutes until the custard is just set.

Remove the pan from the oven and remove custard cups from the water. Allow custards to cool before placing in the refrigerator. Chill overnight.

Two hours before serving, preheat broiler. Sprinkle one tablespoon sugar atop each custard. Place cups on small baking sheet. Caramelize with a blow torch or under a hot grill, rotating sheet for even browning, (about 2 minutes.) Chill until caramelized sugar hardens (about 2 hours.)

(continued)

(Crème Brûlée continued)

Presentation:
Spoon about two tablespoons of the fruit on to each plate.

Tip the ramekin or custard cup upside down on a saucer and then invert saucer to place custard right way up and place on the fruit.   Serve with some raspberry sauce or a sauce of your choice.

Chef's tip:
The Crème Brûlée also tastes nice if you infuse some orange zest or lime zest in the cream when you make the custard.
Thin shortbread cookies are delicious with this dessert.

Bara Brith Pudding

From Hotel Maes-y-Neuadd, Harlech, N. Wales

10 slices of Raisin Bread
½ cup mixed peel
1 teaspoon mixed spice
½ cup golden raisins
3 eggs
1 pint milk
½ cup granulated sugar
¼ cup brown sugar
Oven 300°F

Lightly grease a shallow baking dish and layer it with the sliced bread. Sprinkle with the peel and golden raisins.

Whisk the mixed spice, eggs, sugar and milk together and pour over the bread and sprinkle with brown sugar.

Bake for 1 hour.

Serve hot with whipped cream or ice cream.

Delicious served cold.

Queen of Puddings

1¾ cups fresh white breadcrumbs
Grated peel of one lemon
1 heaped tablespoon sugar
2 cups milk
½ cup softened butter
4 egg yolks
½ teaspoon vanilla extract
3 tablespoons raspberry jam

Put the breadcrumbs, lemon peel and sugar into a mixing bowl. Bring the milk and butter to just below boiling over medium heat. Pour on top of the breadcrumb mixture and allow to stand for 5 minutes.

Grease a 9" soufflé dish and pour in the mixture. Bake for 25 minutes or until the pudding is firm to the touch.

Remove the pudding from the oven and set aside to cool for 5 minutes. Spread the jam on top.

Meringue Topping
3 egg whites
2/3 cup sugar
Oven 350°F

Beat the egg whites until they are stiff and add half the sugar and vanilla. Continue beating until they form firm peaks. Fold in the remaining sugar with a metal spoon and pile on top of the pudding.

Return the pudding to the oven and cook for an additional 15 minutes or until the meringue is slightly brown.

Rothley Court Hotel, Rothley, Leicestershire

Rothley Court's continuous recorded history begins with a mention in the Doomsday Book of 1086, although originally a Roman villa existed on the site.

The holy order of the Knights Templar, founded in 1118 by Hugh de Payens with the aim of protecting pilgrims visiting the Christian shrines of Jerusalem, began acquiring property in England.

The Order possessed a house in the city of Leicester and shortly thereafter was granted land at Rothley by John D Harecourt in 1203 and the Manor House by Henry III in 1228. They built their chapel here, which today stands next to the current Manor House

The Hotel's coat of arms is that of the celebrated Babington family, who bought Rothley Temple and its land around 1550 and held them for nearly 300 years. The motto, translated as 'Faith is all', was repeatedly said to Henry V on the eve of the Battle of Agincourt in 1415 by Thomas Babington, a squire on the King's personal staff.

(continued)

(Rothley Court Hotel, continued)

Thomas Babington was born in this building in 1800 and this famous literary figure later took the title Baron Macaulay of Rothley.

In the 18th Century, William Wilberforce drafted his 'Treaty for the Abolition of Slavery' whilst staying at this court.

In 1893, ownership passed into the hands of the Mertens, who added the south and kitchen wings, and created a splendid Billiards room (now the Wilberforce Room), together with the Lodge, Entrance Gate and Stables.

Ownership subsequently passed to Clive Wormleighton, a member of the modern Order who became Preceptor of Leicester in 1974. He converted the Manor House into a Hotel and Restaurant in 1960 and since this conversion the Rothley court has undergone a steady program of modernization and extension and today there exists a combination of the best of old and new.

The hotel houses a beautiful tapestry in the reception area, and two stained glass windows depicting knights can be seen.

Phone: 011 44 116 237 4141   Fax: 011 44 116 237 4483

Caramel Custard

from Rothley Court Hotel, Rothley, Leicestershire

Serves 4 - 6
Caramel:
3 oz sugar
¼ cup water

Custard:
4 eggs
1 ½ oz sugar
1 pt milk
Few drops of vanilla essence
Oven 325°F

Caramel:
Put the sugar into a heavy pan with water and bring it to the boil. Continue boiling until sugar is golden brown, stirring frequently.

Pour a tablespoon of the caramel into molds (custard cups or 6 inch ramekins) and make sure the bases are evenly covered.

When cool, butter the sides of the molds.

Custard:
Blend together the eggs and sugar. Warm the milk and pour it on to the egg mixture. Mix well and add a few drops of vanilla essence. Strain the custard into the molds. Place them in a baking dish half filled with hot water. Bake in a very moderate oven for about 1 hour or until a knife inserted in the centers comes out clean.

Refrigerate overnight before turning them out on to a flat serving dish.

Americans know this dessert as Flan.

Spotted Dick

This steamed pudding originally known as Spotted Dough has raisins in it, hence the name. Serve with hot custard (see note on page 121).

Serves 4 - 6
1 cup flour
1 cup shortening
1 cup freshly made white breadcrumbs
¾ cup raisins
¾ cup currants
5 tablespoons sugar
Pinch of salt
½ teaspoon mixed spice
½ cup plus 2 tablespoons milk

Mix all the dry ingredients together and add the milk to make a stiff dough. Butter a pudding bowl that holds approximately 5 cups and put the dough in it.

Cover the top of the bowl with a large piece of aluminum foil. Make a pleat in the center so it can expend with the heat and tie it in place around the rim with string.

Put the bowl on a steamer rack or an inverted saucer in a large saucepan in approximately 3 inches of water, cover and steam for 2½ hours. Check the level of the water from time to time, and add more if necessary.

To serve: remove the foil and run a knife gently around the pudding. Turn onto a serving plate and serve immediately with hot custard.

Jam Roly-Poly

An old-fashioned English suet pudding that is warm, filling, fattening and quite delicious! It looks very similar to a jellyroll, but it is steamed, not cooked in an oven. (The suet has been replaced with shortening in this recipe.)

Serves 6
1½ cups flour
1½ teaspoons baking powder
Salt
¾ cup shortening
Approximately ¾ cup of equal amounts of milk and water
1 cup raspberry or strawberry jam

Mix the flour, baking powder and a pinch of salt with the shortening in a mixing bowl. Stir in enough of the milk/water to make a stiff dough.

Form the dough into a ball and roll it out in the shape of a rectangle on a well-floured surface. It should be approximately 10 inches long and 4 inches wide. Moisten the edges with a little water.

Spread the jam over the pastry, keeping it about one inch away from each edge.

Roll the pastry so that it looks like a long log and try not to let any of the jam seep out. Press the edges tightly together and wrap the Roly-Poly in aluminum foil. Make 2 or 3 pleats in the foil so that the pudding has room to expand and tie both ends with a piece of string.

Half fill a large saucepan with boiling water and place the Roly-Poly in it. Cover and boil for 2 hours, adding water if necessary to keep the pan half full.

Remove the pudding from the saucepan and allow it to cool slightly before unwrapping the foil. Slide the Roly-Poly on to a warm plate.

Slice and serve with lots of custard (page 121) .

Poor Knights of Windsor Pudding

This is a dish associated with the Berkshire town of Windsor. The name of this very simple, venerable old pudding has a certain frugal grandeur, for it transforms meager stale bread into a delicious rich dessert.

The Poor Knights of Windsor was a military order formed by King Edward III in the fourteenth century. The intention of the king with regard to the poor knights was to, "provide relief and comfortable subsistence for such valiant soldiers as happened in their old age to fall into poverty and decay."

> *Serves 4 - 6*
> *2 cups raspberries*
> *3 tablespoons confectioners' sugar*
> *1 cup heavy cream*
> *½ cup sherry or wine,*
> *3 egg yolks, lightly beaten*
> *6-8 slices bread, crusts removed, cut into triangles*
> *3 ounces butter*
> *1 teaspoon cinnamon*

Use fresh raspberries when in season, or you can substitute with raspberry or strawberry jam.

Sprinkle the raspberries with confectioners' sugar, crush them gently with a fork and set aside. Whip the cream until it is stiff.

Place the sherry or wine in one bowl and the lightly beaten egg yolks in another. Melt the butter in a frying pan and when it is hot, dip the bread slices first in the sherry and then in the egg yolks, then fry the bread on both sides until it is golden brown. Transfer the slices to a warm dish and sprinkle each slice with a little cinnamon.

Place some of the crushed raspberries on each slice of the toasted bread and cover with a spoon of cream.

Serve immediately.

English Summer Pudding

St. Swithin's Day, if thou dost rain
For forty days it will remain.
St. Swithin's Day, if thou be fair
For forty days, 'twill rain no mair.

St. Swithin was an early Saxon Bishop of Winchester who died in 861 AD. St. Swithin's Day falls on July 15th, and according to the rhyme, if it rains on that day, it will rain for another 40 days.

I thought the summer pudding here would take away all thought of the 'typical' rainy English summer. This was my mother's favorite simple pudding. Every fruit in our berry garden was used.

> *Serves 6*
> *3 pounds mixed berries (frozen works too, without syrup. Use*
> *   any combination of raspberries, red currants and blueberries)*
> *1 cup sugar*
> *8-10 slices white bread, with crusts removed*

Wash and rinse the fruit and remove any stems and leaves. Put in a saucepan, add the sugar and cook over low heat, stirring frequently until the sugar has dissolved.

Grease a 1-quart pudding bowl and line the bottom and sides with all but 3 slices of the bread. Make sure that there are no spaces between the seams: trim the slices so they fit together.

Pour the fruit mixture into the bowl over the bread and cover the top with the remaining slices of bread, which should also be trimmed and fitted together so there are no spaces.

Cover the top of the bowl with a flat plate that fits neatly inside the rim and put a heavy weight on top of the plate. An unopened can of food may be used for this. Refrigerate overnight.

Before serving, remove the plate and run a knife gently around the inside of the bowl. Turn the pudding onto a serving dish.

Lindeth Howe Country House Hotel, Windermere, Cumbria

Lindeth Howe, built in 1879, is set in a beautiful six-acre garden on a hillside with spectacular views of Lake Windermere and the fells beyond.

Beatrix Potter, the world-renowned author of 'Peter Rabbit', who fell in love with the place, once owned this famous, highly rated country house. It was here that she wrote and illustrated several of her world-renowned children's stories including 'Pigling Bland'.

Lindeth Howe has subsequently been tastefully developed and extended to become an elegant hotel with an enviable reputation for fine food and attentive service.

Phone: 011 44 15394 45759   Fax: 011 44 15394 46368

Bread and Butter Pudding

from Chef Paul White Lindeth Howe Country House,
Windermere, Cumbria

> *6 slices of whole meal bread with crusts removed*
> *1/3 cup soft butter*
> *1 cup currants*
> *3 eggs plus yolk from 2 more eggs*
> *½ pint milk*
> *¼ pint double cream*
> *Grated rind of 1 lemon*
> *¼ cup dry sherry*
> *¾ cup white sugar*
> *½ teaspoon grated nutmeg*
> *½ cup Apricot jam*
> *Oven 350°F*

Grease a one quart pie dish and arrange currants evenly on the bottom and add the sherry. Butter the bread and arrange on top butter side up.

Beat the eggs, egg yolk, sugar, cream and milk together and stir in the lemon. Pour the liquid over the bread and leave to stand for an hour.

Sprinkle top of the pudding with nutmeg just before placing it in a pre-heated oven.

Bake for 40 – 50 minutes or until custard is set. Leave to cool.

Heat Apricot jam with 2 teaspoons water and pour over top of pudding.

Serve with vanilla ice cream.

White Chocolate Mousse

From Tinakilly House, County Wicklow, Ireland

½ pound white chocolate
1 pint whipping cream
2 ounces sugar

Melt the chocolate in a double saucepan. Whip the cream and add the sugar.

Add ¼ of the cream to the chocolate. Replace over the heat and stir until smooth.

Let cool and stir in the rest of the cream. Pour into custard cups or small dishes. Serve chilled.

Simple Rice Pudding

Serves 4 to 6
1 cup long-grain rice
2 cups water
1/2 teaspoon salt
5 cups whole milk
3/4 cup sugar
1 teaspoon vanilla
ground cinnamon

In a saucepan, bring water and salt to a boil. Add rice, cover pot and reduce heat to a simmer, allowing rice to cook until water is absorbed.

Stir milk and sugar into the rice and allow it to cook uncovered over medium heat for 30 to 40 minutes. Stir frequently until the rice resembles a creamy consistency. Remove from heat and stir in vanilla.

Serve the rice pudding warm or cold and sprinkle with cinnamon.

Chilled Coconut Rice Pudding

From Senior Sous Chef Ian Coleman
The Moat House, Acton Trussell, Stafford

Serves 6
1 cup short grain rice
6   cups milk
4   tablespoons sugar
1   teaspoons coconut liqueur
2   teaspoons freshly grated coconut

Wash rice and place in a thick bottom saucepan. Add milk and sugar and cook on low heat for one hour or until rice is cooked.

Add Liqueur and coconut and leave to set in refrigerator overnight.

Place cold rice in metal rings. Dust the top with icing sugar and glaze with a burner.

Serve with ice cream.

Samosas

3 sheets Filo Pastry
4 fresh Mango, peeled and sliced
1 ounce fresh Ginger sliced thinly
1 stick of melted butter

Cook ginger and mango until soft. Leave to cool.

Brush 2in squares of 3 sheets thick Filo pastry with clarified butter. Place the mango mix on the middle and fold over into triangles and seal edges.

Deep fry until crispy and dust with icing sugar. Serve immediately with the rice pudding and ice cream.

Warm Chocolate Fudge Brownie
with White Chocolate Sorbet and Espresso Sauce.
from Ian Coleman, Senior Sous Chef,
The Moat House, Acton Trussell, Stafford

¾ stick butter
1 cup sugar
4½ ounce dark chocolate
1 tablespoon light molasses
2 eggs
½ cup plain flour
2 tablespoons cocoa powder
½ teaspoon baking powder
Oven 350ºF

White chocolate sorbet
¼ pint water
1 cup sugar
½ pound white chocolate

Espresso sauce
6 egg yolks
½ cup sugar
1 pint milk
1 small cup espresso coffee

Lightly grease an 8 inch cake tin. Put butter, sugar, dark chocolate and molasses in a heavy based saucepan. Heat gently and mix until blended. Remove from heat.

Beat eggs, whisk in the chocolate mixture. Sieve flour, cocoa and baking powder and fold into egg and chocolate mixture.

Pour into cake tin and bake for 25 minutes until top is slightly crispy. Chill before cutting.

White chocolate sorbet: Boil the water and sugar together, add broken white chocolate, stir until melted and churn in ice cream maker until set.

Espresso sauce: Make crème anglaise by whisking sugar and eggs together. Bring the milk to the boil then slowly pour on to the egg and sugar, mixing thoroughly. Put back on to the heat and cook out until sauce thickens. Pour the coffee in and mix. Chill.

To serve: Warm through the brownie, stencil plate with the sauce, place brownie on top. Serve with the sorbet.

Index of Recipes (Alphabetical)

Index of Hotels, Manor Houses & Inns